Health Care Reform Act

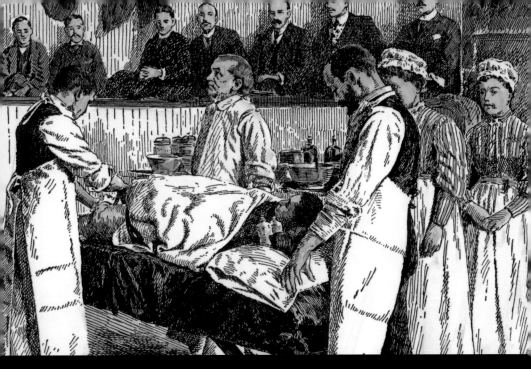

LANDMARK LEGISLATION

Health Care
Reform Act

Susan Dudley Gold

Marshall Cavendish
Benchmark
New York

Dedicated to Ernest Merritt, III, and the members of the
Chronic Pain Support Group of Southern Maine
With thanks to Catherine McGlone, Esq., for her expert review of this manuscript.

Copyright © 2012 Susan Dudley Gold
Published by Marshall Cavendish Benchmark
An imprint of Marshall Cavendish Corporation

This publication represents the opinions and views of the author based on Susan Dudley Gold's personal experience, knowledge, and research. The information in this book serves as a general guide only. The author and publisher have used their best efforts in preparing this book and disclaim liability rising directly and indirectly from the use and application of this book.

Other Marshall Cavendish Offices:
Marshall Cavendish International (Asia) Private Limited, 1 New Industrial Road, Singapore 536196 • Marshall Cavendish International (Thailand) Co Ltd. 253 Asoke, 12th Flr, Sukhumvit 21 Road, Klongtoey Nua, Wattana, Bangkok 10110, Thailand • Marshall Cavendish (Malaysia) Sdn Bhd, Times Subang, Lot 46, Subang Hi-Tech Industrial Park, Batu Tiga, 40000 Shah Alam, Selangor Darul Ehsan, Malaysia

Marshall Cavendish is a trademark of Times Publishing Limited

All websites were available and accurate when this book was sent to press.

Library of Congress Cataloging-in-Publication Data
Gold, Susan Dudley.
The Health Care Reform Act / Susan Dudley Gold.
p. cm. — (Landmark legislation)
Includes bibliographical references and index.
Summary: "Examines United States legislation that has changed policies and implementation of laws regarding American citizens' rights"—Provided by publisher.
ISBN 978-1-60870-486-6 (Print) ISBN 978-1-60870-708-9 (eBook)
1. United States. Patient Protection and Affordable Care Act. 2. National health insurance—Law and legislation—United States—History. 3. Health insurance—Law and legislation—United States—History. 4. Health care reform—United States—History. 5. Medical care—Law and legislation—United States. 6. National health insurance—Law and legislation—United States. 7. Health insurance—Law and legislation—United States. 8. Health care reform—United States. 9. Medicare—Law and legislation. I. Title.
KF3605.G65 2012
344.7302'2—dc22
2010042479

Publisher: Michelle Bisson
Art Director: Anahid Hamparian
Series Designer: Sonia Chaghatzbanian
Photo research by Custom Communications, Inc.

Cover: Democrats in the House march to the Capitol Building in Washington, D.C., for the health care reform vote March 21, 2010. Speaker of the House Nancy Pelosi, center, carries the gavel used when the House passed Medicare in 1965; p. 2: A medical team at Crouse Hospital in Syracuse uses a robot to operate on a patient in 2011; p. 3: Woodcut showing surgery performed at Bellevue Hospital, New York City, in the 1890s.
The photographs in this book are used by permission and through the courtesy of: Getty Images: Chip Somodevilla: cover, 67 (right); 45; Time & Life Pictures, 56; Toni L. Sandys/ The Washington Post, 67 (left). The Image Works: Syracuse Newspapers/Peter Chen, 2; World History/TopFoto, 14. North Wind Picture Archives: 3. AP Images: J. Scott Apple-white, 6; 32, 59; FCC, 62; George Widman, 77; Doug Mills, 83, 84; Mark Wilson, 89; The Indianapolis Star, Frank Espich, 92; John Bazemore, 105; Charles Dharapak, 115; Scott Sady, 118. Library of Congress: 18, 22, 40. Corbis: Bettmann, 60. Landov: Dennis Brack, 68, 74.
[illegible] a (T)

Contents

Democratic members of the House and Senate and others gather around as President Barack Obama signs the Health Care Reform Act into law on March 23, 2010. Among the other onlookers (*from left*): Vice President Joe Biden, Victoria Kennedy, House Speaker Nancy Pelosi, and Senate Majority Leader Harry Reid. The boy on the left is Marcelas Owens, who spoke at a Capitol Hill press conference supporting the bill. The eleven-year-old's mother died after she lost her job because of illness and was forced to give up her health insurance.

Answering the "Call of History"

In 1912 President Theodore Roosevelt's newly formed Progressive Party called for voting rights for women, an eight-hour work day, a ban on child labor, safe workplace conditions—and national health insurance for workers. Roosevelt lost that election and the Progressive Party disbanded several years later. However, almost all of the Progressive issues were implemented into legislation during the twentieth century. Women won the right to vote in 1920. Congress passed laws requiring an eight-hour workday beginning in 1916 and set rigid rules on child labor. The Public Contracts Act of 1936 set safety standards in the workplace, followed by the Occupational Safety and Health Act in 1970, which established stiff penalties for all businesses operating under unsafe conditions.

Roosevelt's call for national health care, however, went unheeded for almost one hundred years—until March 23, 2010, when President Barack Obama signed the Patient Protection and Affordable Care Act into law.

community health centers and helps decrease the cost of prescription medicines for older Americans.

Americans remain sharply divided on the law and the proper role of the federal government in health care. Its opponents continue to work to repeal the law. Federal judges have issued opposite rulings on the law's constitutionality. The matter will most likely end up in the U.S. Supreme Court, where the justices will decide whether to strike down the law or let it stand. Even its strongest advocates concede that the law falls short of providing health care for everyone. Millions of undocumented immigrants do not qualify for health benefits under the law. However, it does represent a major step forward in making medical services accessible to many more Americans.

After the House gave final approval to the bill, President Obama called the vote "a victory for the American People [and] . . . for common sense," and said the legislation moved the nation "decisively in the right direction." Acknowledging that the new law would not solve all the country's health care problems, the president nonetheless noted that the passage represented "another stone firmly laid in the foundation of the American Dream. Tonight," he told American citizens, "we answered the call of history."

Answering the "Call of History"

In 1912 President Theodore Roosevelt's newly formed Progressive Party called for voting rights for women, an eight-hour work day, a ban on child labor, safe workplace conditions—and national health insurance for workers. Roosevelt lost that election and the Progressive Party disbanded several years later. However, almost all of the Progressive issues were implemented into legislation during the twentieth century. Women won the right to vote in 1920. Congress passed laws requiring an eight-hour workday beginning in 1916 and set rigid rules on child labor. The Public Contracts Act of 1936 set safety standards in the workplace, followed by the Occupational Safety and Health Act in 1970, which established stiff penalties for all businesses operating under unsafe conditions.

Roosevelt's call for national health care, however, went unheeded for almost one hundred years—until March 23, 2010, when President Barack Obama signed the Patient Protection and Affordable Care Act into law.

Congress passed the bill to address health care issues that continue to plague the nation. Almost 50 million Americans today have no health insurance and little access to adequate medical care. The new law will eventually include most Americans in health insurance plans. Under the law, almost all citizens and documented immigrants will be required to have health insurance. Employers will pay some of the costs, and government subsidies will help cover premiums for poor Americans. By spreading the cost among many more people, the plan aims to make health care affordable—and accessible—to almost all Americans.

In addition, the health care reform act prohibits insurers from refusing to cover people with preexisting medical conditions or charging them extra fees. That means a person who has battled cancer can purchase the same insurance provided to people with no history of disease. The law bars insurance companies from canceling the policies of those who get sick. It requires companies to continue to provide young adults with coverage on their families' policies until they turn twenty-six. It also requires new insurance plans to cover preventive care services with no extra fees, including immunizations, cancer screenings, and annual doctors' checkups.

Insurers will no longer be allowed to cut off benefits once policy holders reach a certain dollar limit or refuse health insurance to people considered poor health risks. The act outlaws such practices; some were ended in 2010, others were scheduled to be banned in 2014.

For nearly a century, universal health care advocates made repeated attempts to enact a national health insurance plan in the United States. But every effort to expand coverage to all Americans through a federal plan fell short—until 2010.

Until then, well-financed organizations representing doctors, hospitals, dentists, insurance companies, and other businesses ran successful campaigns to defeat health insurance plans overseen by the government. Conservatives in both political parties opposed any federal government role in American health care despite the fact that all other developed countries in the world provided their citizens with national health care plans. Multimillion-dollar advertising campaigns distorted provisions in proposed legislation and played to Americans' fears.

The Patient Protection and Affordable Care Act, informally known as the health care reform act, faced many of the same foes in its journey through Congress. This time, however, a president dedicated to the cause, a Democratic-controlled Congress, a determined House speaker, and skillful political maneuvers and compromises pushed the bill through to become a law. It became the first major piece of legislation in recent memory to pass without one Republican vote, an indication of the bitter divide over the health plan. Passage of the bill represented a huge step forward in the century-long effort during which presidents of both parties tried and failed to win health insurance coverage for Americans.

The Patient Protection and Affordable Care Act ensures that more than 95 percent of Americans will be covered by health insurance by 2014. It expands coverage to include more than 32 million citizens who previously had no insurance coverage. The new legislation provides tax credits and subsidies to low- and middle-income families and to small businesses that offer health benefits to their workers. Exchanges set up under the law's provisions will provide competitive health insurance plans for people and employers in all states to choose from. The legislation also earmarks $11 billion for community health centers and helps decrease the cost of prescription medicines for older Americans.

Americans remain sharply divided on the law and the proper role of the federal government in health care. Its opponents continue to work to repeal the law. Federal judges have issued opposite rulings on the law's constitutionality. The matter will most likely end up in the U.S. Supreme Court, where the justices will decide whether to strike down the law or let it stand. Even its strongest advocates concede that the law falls short of providing health care for everyone. Millions of undocumented immigrants do not qualify for health benefits under the law. However, it does represent a major step forward in making medical services accessible to many more Americans.

After the House gave final approval to the bill, President Obama called the vote "a victory for the American People [and] . . . for common sense," and said the legislation moved the nation "decisively in the right direction." Acknowledging that the new law would not solve all the country's health care problems, the president nonetheless noted that the passage represented "another stone firmly laid in the foundation of the American Dream. Tonight," he told American citizens, "we answered the call of history."

Health Care Reform Act Provisions

BENEFITS

- Insurance coverage for almost all Americans.
- Competitive private insurance market (state exchanges) providing affordable coverage.
- Subsidies to help pay premiums for Americans who don't qualify for health insurance or can't afford it.
- Tax credits for small businesses who provide workers' health benefits and subsidies for firms that cover retirees' insurance.
- Rebates ($250 in 2010) and increased drug benefits under Medicare.
- Increased benefits under Medicaid and expansion of the program to cover all Americans under age sixty-five who fall within certain income guidelines.
- Emergency care covered without higher copays.
- Free annual checkups and preventive care services.
- Home and community services for people with disabilities.

PAYMENTS

- Excise tax on insurers' most expensive benefits plans.
- Excise tax on indoor tanning salons.
- New fees for pharmaceutical companies, medical device manufacturers, and insurance companies. (They benefit from increased business from new customers.)

- Higher Medicare payroll taxes for wealthy Americans (those earning more than $200,000 a year).

INSURANCE COMPANY RULES
- Allow young Americans up to age twenty-six to be covered under their parents' policies.
- Submit proposed rate hikes to state agencies for review.
- Provide coverage for all with no extra charges for pre-existing conditions, gender, or other factors.
- Stop canceling policies when people become ill.
- Eliminate lifetime or annual caps on benefits.
- Spend 80 to 85 percent of income from policies on health care or pay the excess back to policy holders.

INDIVIDUAL/EMPLOYER RULES
- All citizens and legal residents must have health insurance by 2014 or pay an annual fee ($95 in 2014, increasing to $695 in 2016).
- Employers with more than fifty workers who do not provide a health insurance program for their workers have to pay $2,000 for each employee if any full-time worker receives federally subsidized health insurance (first thirty employees are exempt when figuring fee).
- Employers who offer plans for their workers have to pay $3,000 for each employee who receives federally subsidized health insurance (or $2,000 per worker, whichever is less).

Cost of plan: $940 billion over ten years.
Effect on deficit: Projected to reduce the deficit by $143 billion* over ten years.

* Source: Congressional Budget Office, March 2010

CHAPTER ONE

Taking Care of the Sick

In colonial America, health care was rudimentary at best. Many of the early settlers who became ill died for lack of treatment. Childhood was an especially risky period of life. Conditions were harsh, and there were no immunizations against diseases such as mumps and measles, which often proved fatal.

The colonies had few doctors or other trained medical personnel. Those who practiced medicine did not have to pass tests, attend special schools, or be certified. Most colonial doctors were well-educated by the standards of the day; the majority learned their skills from experienced local doctors, though some emigrated from Europe or studied abroad. Those who provided medical care in the rural areas were usually less educated, with little or no formal medical training. They traveled in horse and buggy to their patients' homes, sometimes riding many miles in a single day. These traveling, or itinerant, doctors opened up shop in residences and advertised their services on flyers or by word of mouth.

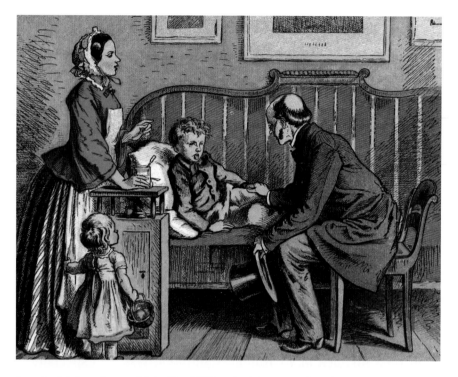

In colonial America and into the 1900s, doctors treated patients in their homes. Even after hospitals were established, many doctors continued to make home visits.

Most households relied on their own folk remedies to treat illness. In towns, barber and apothecary shops provided some medical treatment—barbers pulled teeth, for example. A local "herb lady" or healer might also offer remedies for illness, with some performing amputations, and resorting to other drastic treatment.

Even when well-trained doctors provided the treatment, their methods were little more effective than those of the local healers. Scientists had not yet discovered the role of bacteria and viruses in causing infection, or the need for sanitary equipment and cleanliness while treating patients. Doctors had access to few effective medicines, so they relied instead on herbs, folk remedies, homemade concoctions, and various elixirs imported from Europe. Sufferers had little besides a slug of whiskey or sometimes opium or quinine to help ease pain. Doctors did not perform lengthy surgeries on patients until the 1800s and only did so on a routine basis after the 1840s, when ether began to be used as an anesthetic.

FIRST HOSPITALS

In 1751 Dr. Thomas Bond, an American-born Quaker, and Benjamin Franklin established one of the nation's first hospitals in Philadelphia in 1752. It became the institution's mission "to care for the sick-poor and insane who were wandering the streets of Philadelphia." The first patients were admitted for treatment in the newly completed institution in 1756. Benjamin Rush, known as America's first psychiatrist, established more humane treatment for patients with mental illnesses at the hospital, beginning in 1783.

Several other hospitals opened their doors in U.S. cities over the next ninety years. The hospitals fell into two categories: those founded by private, charitable organizations and those chartered by local or regional governments. A number of institutions focused on treatment for a particular disease or specialty or treated only people in a certain category.

During much of the 1800s, however, few people outside urban areas had access to hospitals. Wealthier citizens hired private doctors to treat them in their homes or traveled to facilities in the city. Those with no money sought treatment at infirmaries attached to poorhouses. The working poor and middle-class citizens unable to afford expensive, out-of-state hospital care had nowhere to go when they developed health problems the local doctor could not treat.

Ironically, it was war that led to better health care for the general population. The Civil War brought with it widespread death and destruction. Thousands of soldiers died in the field from their wounds or from disease and infection. Clara Barton, who would later establish the American Red Cross, was among the many citizens who took care of the soldiers on the battlegrounds and lobbied to get them better treatment.

From the first military hospital with 250 beds, temporary facilities quickly appeared throughout the war-torn country. One such hospital in Richmond, Virginia, housed 7,000 patients in wooden barracks. To keep patients fed, the Richmond facility had its own cows, goats, and even a bakery—although this sounds strange today, it was not uncommon in early hospitals. These temporary hospitals erected near the battlefronts became models for general public hospitals.

Following the Civil War, the need for public hospitals grew as workers flocked to factories in the newly emerging cities of the North. People lived in overcrowded, dirty tenements, in cities where raw sewage and horse dung filled the streets. Such conditions bred contagious, often deadly, diseases, including tuberculosis, pneumonia, and typhoid fever. Workers hardy enough to withstand disease often died, or were maimed, in industrial accidents.

BETTER TRAINING FOR DOCTORS

As the population grew, the need for more doctors increased. Philadelphia chartered the first medical school in the colonies in 1765 at the University of Pennsylvania, followed by Columbia University in 1767, Pennsylvania State in 1769, and Harvard University in 1783. By 1820 America had thirteen medical schools. Additionally, after nurses demonstrated their skill on the battlefields of the Civil War, the first training schools for nurses opened in 1872 at the New England

Hospital for Women and Children in Boston and the Women's Hospital Training School for Nurses in Philadelphia.

In 1848, a group of doctors founded the American Medical Association (AMA) to set standards for the medical profession. The group monitored its members and helped establish criteria for medical schools and the practice of medicine.

Despite the advent of the AMA, the prevalence of quack remedies, which did at least as much harm as good, and of unsanitary practices in hospitals continued through the late 1800s. A major breakthrough in medicine came in the 1850s when French chemist Louis Pasteur discovered that bacteria causes disease. His finding led to the pasteurization of milk, preventing it from spreading illness, and eventually to vaccinations for such contagious diseases as typhoid, malaria, and tuberculosis. In the 1860s the Quaker physician Joseph Lister applied Pasteur's theory to medical practice by disinfecting all surgical instruments, wounds, and the surgeons' hands with carbolic acid before and after surgery.

But not all doctors of the time accepted Lister's conclusions about germs. Dr. Stephen H. Weeks, a distinguished surgeon and professor of anatomy and surgery at Maine's two medical schools, referred to "the germ *theory* of disease" in a paper he wrote in 1889 and acknowledged that he was "not a complete convert to Listerism."

Other doctors, however, pushed for better sterilization methods. By the 1880s, hospitals took precautions on a regular basis to prevent germs from infecting patients. Medical staff members began to routinely disinfect surgical instruments with steam and sterilize their hands and other exposed areas with disinfectants. The Johns Hopkins Hospital, founded in Baltimore in 1889, became the first to base treatment and research on the scientific method, which

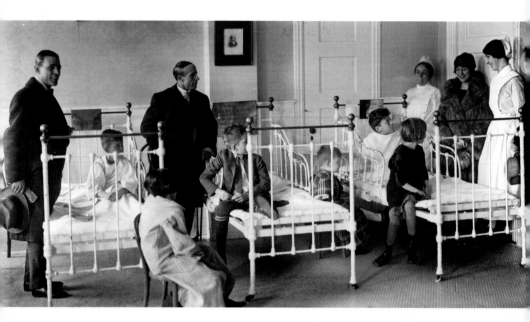

Doctors and nurses visit child patients at the New York Post-Graduate Medical School and Hospital around 1920.

required objective examination and testing of theories. It also was a pioneer in adopting new procedures, such as requiring staff members to wear rubber gloves during surgery.

The number of hospitals in the United States mushroomed from 178 in 1873 to more than 2,500 at the end of the nineteenth century. As widespread use of sterilization measures became the norm and death rates at hospitals declined, people shifted their views of medical institutions as places of death to places of treatment. By the early 1900s hospitals had replaced the home as the place to seek medical care.

MEDICAL ADVANCES
The twentieth century ushered in monumental advances in medicine, technology, and lifestyle. In 1900 American scientist R. A. Fessenden spoke the first words transmitted

Early Hospitals

During its first year of operation, in 1874, Maine General Hospital in Portland, Maine, admitted almost everyone who appeared at its doors. Once the hospital was established, those with chronic illnesses had to seek treatment elsewhere. Admitting those with lingering diseases for which there was no cure would take away beds needed by many others who could be treated. Maine General also refused admission to people with highly contagious diseases.

Subscribers paid into a fund that helped finance medical care for the poor. Poor people could occupy a hospital bed for free, or at a reduced rate if they were able to pay a portion of the fee, for up to three months. A longer stay had to be approved by the board of directors.

Donors could designate who would use the hospital beds they paid for. Businesses secured beds for employees and their families. If the person or business paying for the bed did not need it, the hospital could use it for other patients.

Patients who could not pay for medical care were assigned duties while in the hospital. Those who could do so were directed to help other patients or assist the resident physician or matron (supervisor in charge of the hospital's domestic affairs) with chores when asked. A refusal could lead to dismissal from the hospital by the Visiting Committee.

over radio waves. The rest of that decade would prove to be remarkable: the Wright brothers successfully flew a motor-powered airplane; electricity replaced steam as America's primary energy source; the Panama Canal was built; and Henry Ford opened the Ford Motor Company and began production of the Model T, the first mass-produced car.

This age of technological advances and global communication dramatically affected medicine. During the early 1900s, scientists invented the ultramicroscope (a super-microscope powerful enough to view microscopic particles) and the electrocardiograph (a machine that records the heart's electrical activity); American doctors eradicated yellow fever in the Panama Canal Zone; and Marie Curie won the Nobel Prize for her work in radioactivity. Researchers began delving into the study of genetics, and Sigmund Freud published works on human sexuality and the mind.

With advances in medical equipment and technology came the need for improved hospital facilities, as well as rising costs. Hospitals coped with the financial demands in various ways. Yale-New Haven Hospital in Connecticut, for example, depended on "modest" rate increases and contributions from donors during the first two decades of the century. The hospital, like many others, had been founded as a charitable institution, and directors balked at putting the full burden of costs on patients. Instead, they balanced the budget by taking out a bond, accepting a $50,000 payment from Yale University for services as a teaching hospital, and setting up a voluntary subscription program, which helped pay for medical care for the poor.

America's first insurance companies were established in the 1750s. In the next century, the Massachusetts Health Insurance Company of Boston offered the first group insurance policy in 1847. During the 1860s, Americans could buy policies that paid benefits in the event of an accident, but only if the injury occurred on a train or a steamboat. By the end of the nineteenth century, insurance companies were selling policies that covered most types of injuries and illnesses. This "sickness" insurance did not cover health care costs, which were low, but instead provided money to replace lost wages when a worker became ill or injured. During this time hospitals began itemizing bills, charging separately for food, surgical dressings, operating room usage, and nursing care.

As medical costs increased and more workers faced hardships after suffering injuries on the job, states took steps to help them. In 1902 Maryland became the first state to pass a worker's compensation law that provided medical care for workers injured on the job. Other states followed, and by 1949 every state had adopted a similar law. The legislation did not cover ill workers or those whose injuries could not be linked to the job. Many states restricted benefits to workers in high-risk professions. Part-timers, the self-employed, and the unemployed received no insurance coverage for medical expenses under workers' compensation laws.

TEDDY ROOSEVELT PITCHES A NATIONAL PLAN

During his unsuccessful bid for another term as president in 1912, Theodore Roosevelt promoted national accident and illness insurance for workers. As Roosevelt and his Progressive Party supporters envisioned it, the insurance would supplement injured and sick workers' income rather than pay for health care costs. Such insurance, Roosevelt noted, should be paid for by businesses, workers, and "perhaps the people at large," who would all contribute toward the premiums. Without such insurance, he said, "the community pays

Theodore Roosevelt (*center*) proposed a plan for national health insurance during the presidential campaign in 1912. He lost the election and the insurance plan failed to win passage in Congress.

a heavy cost in lessened efficiency and in misery." Roosevelt suggested that the United States study Germany's system, which provided pensions for seniors and health insurance for workers, as a model for its own. Germany first implemented mandatory accident and illness insurance, paid for by employers for their workforce, in 1883. By 1912, most European powers had adopted some form of national health insurance or subsidized health insurance paid for by workers themselves.

Roosevelt lost the election, and the Progressives' pitch for national health insurance faltered along with the party. But even after Roosevelt's defeat at the polls, reformers in the American Association for Labor Legislation (AALL) pushed for compulsory health insurance at the state level. The organization, founded in 1906 by a group of economists, promoted uniform laws to improve labor conditions and make the workplace safer. They believed that improving the lot of workers would make businesses more efficient. Among AALL's most prominent members were Louis D. Brandeis, legal expert and later U.S. Supreme Court justice; Jane Addams, Nobel Prize–winning social worker; Woodrow Wilson, Princeton University president who later became president of the United States; Edward A. Filene, founder of Filene's department store; labor leader Samuel Gompers, founder of the American Federation of Labor (AFL); and James M. Lynch, New York's commissioner of labor.

AALL formed a national committee to study the need for health insurance and held America's first national conference on health insurance in 1913. In 1915 the group developed a proposed bill to be presented to the state legislatures that called for compulsory health insurance for America's workers. The plan, based on the national health programs of Great Britain and Germany, guaranteed workers who earned $1,200 a year or less—including those who worked part-time or at home—free medical services, sick pay, and medicine if they were injured or ill. States would pay one-fifth of the cost of the premiums, with employers and employees sharing the remaining expense. The insurance plan would also pay for preventive care such as annual physicals and inoculations, as well as medical treatment. Self-employed workers and those who worked without pay for family businesses could voluntarily obtain state-regulated insurance policies under the plan.

The AALL proposal covered only workers in private businesses or those employed by local and state entities, not their families and not those employed by the federal government. Proponents of the plan reasoned that restricting benefits to workers would put fewer burdens on taxpayers and would allow statisticians to determine more easily whether the cost of health insurance for workers was offset by the benefit to industry. Advocates argued that the insurance plan would reduce long absences from work (helping employers as well as employees), prevent the spread of illness, and keep sick workers from falling into poverty. Statistics on workers' health in the 1910s revealed that illness and injury annually cost American workers $180 million in medical care and $500 million in lost wages.

Inspired by the AALL model bill, California set up a commission to study the proposal in 1915. The following year the governors of California, Massachusetts, and Nevada urged the passage of health insurance legislation. The governors of New Hampshire and Wisconsin called for commissions to investigate the proposal.

DOCTORS OBJECT

At first the American Medical Association endorsed the idea. The editor of the *Journal of the American Medical Association* wrote of the plan in an article published in 1916, "No other social movement in modern economic development is so pregnant with benefit to the public." *JAMA* advised its physician readers to "study this important and far-reaching problem and help to work out an equitable method for furnishing relief and medical aid for workingmen."

The AMA's position changed, however, under pressure from many individual doctors who opposed the plan. They feared the insurance plan would make doctors "a servant of the State rather than the possessor of a comfortable private practice." Doctors also objected to the plan's proposal to reorganize doctors into group practices, a system widely used in

Europe. Under such a system, doctors formed a group and shared offices and staff rather than practicing on their own.

Dr. S. S. Goldwater, a member of the AALL Social Insurance Committee that drafted the bill, addressed the doctors' concerns at a meeting of the Medical Society of the County of New York in 1916. He said that many patients waited until their condition was severe, then went to a free clinic for treatment. Under the insurance plan, Goldwater noted, these patients would be able to go to a doctor for early treatment, and doctors would receive payment, which otherwise might not be given. In Great Britain, he said, where national health insurance had been in place since 1911, doctors' incomes rose after the program was adopted. He also noted that the states' financial backing assured that doctors would be paid.

Goldwater predicted that sooner or later the conditions that led to Europe's adoption of national health insurance would force the United States to follow suit. "That the United States should be the last of the great civilized countries of the world to consider this matter seriously is but natural," he said. "We are more individualistic than Europe, and we have been more prosperous; for these reasons we have preferred to allow the industrial worker to shift for himself."

Goldwater noted that Americans had two choices: either let sick workers who could not afford medical care suffer and possibly die or help them pay for the treatment they needed. That help could come in the form of charitable giving or from health insurance, or both. Because the plan set forth in the legislation applied only to workers, Goldwater predicted that Americans would rely on a combination of charity and insurance to deal with the problem. Goldwater said there was strong public demand for the legislation. "The bill will find strong support among all the interested groups, including taxpayers, employers, and industrial workers," he told the medical society.

INSURERS LEAD OPPOSITION

The International Association of Casualty and Surety Underwriters, representing insurance companies, led opposition to the legislation. The bill threatened their business, particularly the sale of insurance to cover burials. Family members would receive a cash payment to cover the burial of a deceased worker covered by the AALL plan. Other businesses expressed skepticism toward the bill. In its trade journal, the Associated Manufacturers and Merchants of New York State criticized the "well meaning but deluded uplifters" for proposing a scheme that would allow "lazy" workers to collect money while engaging in "scientific loafing."

The leaders of the AALL relied on research and data to win support for their bill. They lobbied hard to convince lawmakers and doctors of the plan's value. The reformers unwisely failed to consult labor leaders when drafting the legislation and neglected to build grassroots support among workers or the general public. Some labor leaders feared the bill would undercut unions' efforts to improve benefits for workers.

Nonetheless, many local labor union members embraced the plan, particularly women workers, who applauded the proposal's cash benefit to allow mothers to take time off from work two weeks before the birth of a child and stay home for an additional six weeks after the baby was born. AFL leaders were cool to the plan. Despite his membership in AALL, Samuel Gompers, AFL president, called the legislation "a menace to the rights, welfare, and liberty of American workers" and led a union effort opposing the AALL bill. At its annual meeting in 1918, however, the AFL endorsed the principle of workers' health insurance and ordered the executive council to study the concept and if approved, formulate the organization's own model bill.

Between 1916 and 1920 fourteen state legislatures debated the issue. It seemed that health insurance for workers would soon become a reality, at least in several states. New York, New Jersey, and Massachusetts were the first to consider the bill during the 1916 legislative session. The Massachusetts Legislature held the first hearing on the proposal on March 1, 1916. Irving Fisher, a Yale economist and AALL's president, predicted in December 1916 that the issue of national health insurance would be "a burning question" within the next six months. "At present," he remarked, "the United States has the unenviable distinction of being the only great industrial nation without compulsory health insurance."

Four months later, in 1917, America declared war against Germany. World War I brought the health insurance campaign to an abrupt halt. Critics of the plan quickly labeled the AALL program as "made in Germany." The American public, hostile to all things German, turned against the proposal. By the end of the war, in November 1918, many Americans had adopted the view expressed by New York physician John J. A. O'Reilly that the insurance plan was "UnAmerican, Unsafe, Uneconomic, Unscientific, Unfair, and Unscrupulous."

Nevertheless, the push for health insurance continued. In 1917 six more states set up commissions to study the issue. The following year governors in New Jersey and Massachusetts went on record as supporting compulsory health insurance to promote public health. That year the California Legislature approved an amendment to the state constitution to create a health insurance program for workers. Before the vote on the amendment, a group of insurance companies ran an ad in the San Francisco *Chronicle* that warned the health insurance plan "would spell social ruin to the United States." Opponents also sent pamphlets with the German Kaiser's picture on them to every California voter. The flyers portrayed the health insurance plan as "Born in Germany" and asked readers, "Do you want it in California?" Voters in the state rejected the amendment in November 1918 by a wide margin. The amendment's defeat in California marked the beginning of the end for the AALL plan.

NEW YORK'S FAILED CAMPAIGN

After the California debacle, supporters of the bill focused their efforts on New York. In 1919, after almost four years of debate and the introduction of four separate bills, the New York Senate passed a health insurance bill. Bowing to demands by local physicians, lawmakers amended the original AALL bill to allow those covered by insurance to pick their own doctors, who would then be paid by the plan. Fees would be based on local wage scales for doctors. The plan allowed employees to transfer from one company to another without losing coverage. Managers and company officers, farm workers, and domestic servants were not included in the insurance program. It also did not cover federal, state, and local government employees. The plan was expected to cost employees and employers around 24 cents a week.

The Republican Party dominated both houses of the New York Legislature that session. Although the health insurance measure was part of the "social welfare" reforms in the legislative package proposed by New York's Democratic Governor Alfred E. Smith, Republican State Senator Frederick M. Davenport introduced the Senate version of the bill. Dissidents in the Republican Party joined with Democrats to pass the legislation in the Senate. But Republicans in the New York Assembly, the state's House of Representatives, rejected almost all the reforms, including the health insurance bill.

The loss in New York dealt a crushing blow to the AALL effort. Supporters had hoped passage of the bill in New York would spur Massachusetts and other states to enact their own health insurance legislation, with the ultimate goal of a national health insurance program. Commissions in a number of states issued reports urging the adoption of health insurance laws. None of them, however, resulted in state laws mandating health insurance.

A second health insurance bill introduced by Senator Davenport in the next session of the New York Legislature also went down in defeat. Representatives from the League of Women Voters, the State Federation of Labor, the New York City Department of Health, and a Republican women's group spoke in favor of the proposal, while business groups, local chambers of commerce, medical professionals, and individual manufacturers opposed it. The AALL waged similar campaigns in several other states, all of which failed to win passage of a health insurance law. The group folded in 1943, but not before it had made major changes in the way Americans regarded health care and the idea of health insurance.

"A DEAD ISSUE"

The battle over the state health insurance bills foreshadowed the fight advocates would face over the next ninety years every time the proposal for compulsory health insurance resurfaced. Advocates on both sides made liberal use of rhetoric. Opponents speaking before the New York Senate Labor and Industrial Committee denounced the health insurance proposal as "pernicious and un-American." Other opponents of the plan called it a plot by socialists to do away with America's free enterprise system.

Those who supported the plan leveled scathing criticisms of their own against the opposition. A leader in the Republican women's group in New York likened words spoken by an opponent of the plan to "Bolshevist [communist] propaganda" and said his role in defeating the measure smacked of "disloyalty toward our Government."

Objections centered around two major concerns: loss of control and loss of income. Doctors argued that under a government-run system of health insurance, they would receive less pay for their services, be forced to join group practices, and have less control over fees and the way they ran their offices. Company executives objected to what they saw as government intrusion in their business and additional costs that would undercut profits. National labor leaders preferred to focus on higher wages and safety issues and wanted workers to view unions—not the government—as their benefactor. Insurance companies feared the bill—which included a modest death benefit—would do away with their burial insurance business.

Support for the bill came from reformers, some labor groups, several women's groups, public health advocates, and others. Their major arguments in favor of health insurance were that it would improve public health, increase productivity of workers, and decrease poverty. Edward H. Lewinski-Corwin of the New York Academy of Medicine argued for the sort of health insurance system that would help ease overcrowding at free clinics and hospital charity wards, where those who could not afford medical care sought treatment. The situation also burdened taxpayers, he noted, who had to foot the bill for state and local aid to hospitals. Louis S.

Reed, an economic analyst whose focus was health care, also argued for health insurance. He noted that Europe's experience with such programs showed that people covered by national health insurance received better medical care than they had before the plans were adopted. Labor leaders promoted the plan as a way to increase productivity by preventing workplace disease and keeping workers healthy. Reformers supported the health insurance proposal as the best way to provide medical services to all and as a means of keeping sick people from sliding into poverty.

Opponents of the bill had the most success in shaping the public's view of government health insurance programs. They portrayed the plan as a big-government, antibusiness scheme that threatened the U.S. medical profession and American independence. Doctors told patients the legislation would prevent them from choosing their own physician, industrialists claimed the plan would hurt business, and national labor leaders contended it would make it harder to win other benefits, such as higher wages and better working conditions. Meanwhile, conservatives championed the belief that it was each individual's responsibility—not that of government—to take care of his or her own needs.

The combination of anti-German propaganda, attacks from the insurance industry, and doctors' opposition turned the American public against the health insurance proposals. In 1920, the AMA adopted a resolution opposing compulsory health insurance. Five years later, New York's medical society concluded that any government health insurance plan was "a dead issue in the United States." The defeat of the AALL plan would shape the development of the U.S. medical system and solidify opposition to universal health insurance for the next ninety years.

President Franklin D. Roosevelt (*center*) dedicates a new medical center in New Jersey in 1936. During his speech, the president assured doctors that the Social Security Act would not be detrimental to the medical profession. Roosevelt refused to include national health care in his Social Security plan because he feared the additional benefit package would kill the bill.

CHAPTER TWO

Health Care— Round Two

For the next decade and a half, advocates made little progress in promoting universal health insurance for Americans. During this time, the cost of medical care rose rapidly. As hospitals adopted new technology and undertook more complex procedures, the cost of construction, equipment, and staff salaries soared. Charities could no longer foot the bill, and hospitals expected patient fees to cover a much larger portion of the costs. Families who had spent only a small portion of their medical bills on hospitalization (about 7.6 percent of the total cost of their health care) in 1918 were faced with higher hospital fees. By 1934, 40 percent of Americans' medical payments went to hospitals.

The first health insurance policies offered limited coverage. Most of those who bought the insurance in the late 1800s sought benefits that covered lost wages rather than medical bills. As medical costs rose, however, sick Americans looked to insurance for help paying doctors and hospitals.

Medical bills became a larger burden for sick workers than lost wages. In an effort to deal with the growing medical debt, Baylor University Hospital in Dallas, Texas, introduced a new payment plan, called the Baylor Plan, in 1929. The plan provided twenty-one days of free medical care at the hospital to subscribers who paid a monthly fee. The first participants, teachers in the Dallas, Texas, school district, paid fifty cents each month, while families paid $1.50. The first patient to collect benefits under the plan, Alma Dickson, was treated for a fractured ankle in December 1929. The plan paid the full cost of her hospital stay. News of the benefit spread, and hospitals across the country joined to form a nonprofit organization under the auspices of the American Hospital Association (AHA), which eventually became known as the Blue Cross Association. By 1939, the insurance group was providing hospital insurance for 3 million Americans.

States let Blue Cross, a nonprofit organization, avoid many of the regulations and tax requirements of profit-making firms. Despite this, several large for-profit insurance companies also began offering group plans for hospital coverage during the 1930s. Both profit and nonprofit insurers negotiated to pay lower rates to hospitals for their services in exchange for guaranteed payments.

For years doctors resisted pressure to participate in insurance plans to cover their fees. They wanted to be able to set their own fees and choose their own patients and feared an insurance plan would reduce their incomes and force them into group practices. In 1936 the editor of the *Journal of the National Medical Association*, the voice of the African American medical community, chided doctors for their reluctance to follow the AHA's lead in setting up an insurance plan. "In this arrangement," he said, "the hospitals have gone all the way across the road, while the doctors have not even left the sidewalk. They must do it. It is a necessity." In 1937 the AMA's House of Delegates approved the hospital plans with the provision that they "should be limited exclusively to hospital facilities" and not include doctors' fees. The delegates passed a similar resolution the following year.

Doctors finally agreed to a prepaid plan similar to the Blue Cross program promoted by the AHA. The program later became known as Blue Shield. It was based on a plan set up by workers in the timber and mining industry on the West Coast. These workers paid groups of local doctors a set fee each month in return for medical care. The first Blue Shield plan began in California in 1939 and became widespread in the late 1940s. Doctors accepted the group plan in part as a way to stall support for a government-sponsored health insurance program. Like the hospitals' Blue Cross program, Blue Shield operated as a nonprofit with exemptions from certain tax and regulatory requirements.

COMMITTEE ON THE COST OF MEDICAL CARE

Despite growing concern over rising medical costs, the AMA passed a resolution in 1920 to oppose any health insurance program run by the government. Disturbed by this dismissal of the issue, a group of doctors in 1926 established a committee to investigate the problem of costly medical care. This Committee of Five laid the groundwork for a larger group to tackle the issue and find solutions. The resultant Committee on the Cost of Medical Care (CCMC) formed in 1927 to study the best way to organize the health care system to make it more efficient and allow more Americans to benefit from it. The group, privately funded and made up of an impressive collection of nearly fifty economists, physicians, and other health-related specialists, published twenty-five weighty reports and dozens of papers on the subject over the next five years.

In its final report, issued in 1932 during the Great Depression, the CCMC concluded that the most efficient and effective way to deliver medical care was by setting up group practices and having state and local agencies coordinate health services. The report endorsed basic public health services for all Americans. It further recommended improvements in education for doctors and others in health-related careers and government programs to prevent disease. The CCMC's proposals relied on voluntary group insurance, taxes, or both to foot the bill for medical care. Individuals would also have the option of paying for select services themselves.

The CCMC recommendations created a stir, even among the group's own members. Several filed minority reports, and at least one member supported compulsory health insurance to provide the funds to expand medical care to Americans. The greatest disagreement arose over the formation of group practices and reliance on group insurance. Eight doctors who filed a minority report firmly opposed any government intervention in health care. Government's only role, they maintained, should be to care for the poor, promote public health, deal with diseases requiring treatment in institutions (such as tuberculosis), and provide medical services for veterans and members of the military. They objected to group practices as "wasteful" and "unfair" to general practitioners with their own offices. The dissenting doctors also objected to group insurance, voluntary or compulsory, because they did not want insurers to encourage competition among doctors to get the best prices for medical services.

The AMA endorsed the doctors' minority report and

attacked the CCMC's call for group insurance and group practices. But before the decade was over, doctors would embrace group insurance. At the end of the century, group practices would flourish in response to economic pressures. In the early 1930s, however, national AMA officers preached against the study's conclusions at medical societies throughout the country. A blistering editorial in the medical society's journal, *JAMA*, described the report as "an incitement to revolution." Outside the medical community, American newspapers joined in criticizing the plan. A front-page story's headline in the *New York Times* referred to the CCMC report as "socialized medicine," and other newspapers published similar critiques of the recommendations.

SOCIAL SECURITY BUT NO HEALTH BENEFITS

AMA opposition and the furor over the report buried any effort to put the CCMC recommendations into action. Time had run out for studies, as the country, deep in the Great Depression, focused on more immediate problems. The newly elected president, Franklin D. Roosevelt, and his team worked feverishly to put together the New Deal, a rescue plan they hoped would lift the nation's economy. As they fashioned the New Deal programs, the negative publicity swirling around the CCMC's proposals hammered home a truth: anyone pursuing the health care issue (and in particular compulsory health insurance) risked drowning in politically dangerous waters, thanks to the opposition of the AMA and others in the medical community.

President Roosevelt presented the Social Security bill to Congress as part of his New Deal package in 1935. The legislation proposed a brand-new system of retirement benefits, managed by the federal government, for most working

Americans. The plan did not cover government workers, most of whom received pensions under a separate system. The new program, called Social Security, would be funded by compulsory group insurance paid for by employers and employees through payroll deductions and taxes—the same system reformers had advocated for years to fund universal health care. Payments to retirees were based on the amount of money they earned during their working career. "I see no reason why every child, from the day he is born, shouldn't be a member of the social security system," Roosevelt told Labor Secretary Frances Perkins, who helped create the bill. "When he begins to grow up, he should know he will have old-age benefits direct from the insurance system to which he will belong all his life."

Advocates of universal health care pushed the administration to include health care coverage in the bill. They argued that it would be simple to extend Social Security's compulsory group insurance to cover health care as well as retirement benefits. Others promoted the idea of extending health benefits to all Americans, not just the elderly. With the Depression still raging, many sick people could not afford to buy medicine, see a doctor, or get treatment at a hospital.

Roosevelt rejected their urgings, however, because he feared that AMA opposition to health insurance would doom the entire measure. Congress passed the Social Security Act in August 1935. It contained a separate provision for unemployment benefits for workers who had lost their jobs—but no provision for health care.

TRUMAN'S HEALTH CARE PLAN

Advocates looked to another New Deal proposal, the Wagner National Health Act of 1939, to win health insurance coverage for Americans. Introduced by Democratic Senator Robert F. Wagner of New York, the bill called for a national health program funded by federal grants and managed by the states and local communities. The 1938 election had brought several conservative members to Congress who did not support the measure. Without much support from Roosevelt, the bill died. The entrance of the United States into World War II in 1941 halted further action on the issue—for a while.

The defeat of his bill sent Senator Wagner and other reformers back to the drawing board. They gained inspiration from a report by William Beveridge on proposals for the British health care system. Beveridge's plan called for a government-run health care system, with taxes paying the bill for comprehensive medical treatment for everyone. Under the plan, the government owned the nation's hospitals, and specialists at the hospitals were on the federal payroll. General practitioners received payment from the government, but they could also collect fees from private patients. Great Britain adopted Beveridge's plan and began operating the National Health Service, with medical services available to all at no charge, in 1948. Since then, many other countries have adopted plans based on the Beveridge system.

In 1943 Wagner and two other Democrats, Senator James Murray of Montana and Representative John Dingell of Michigan, introduced a joint bill that expanded Social Security benefits to include medical care. A poll conducted by *Fortune* magazine in 1942 had shown that 74 percent of those questioned favored a national plan to provide health care. The joint bill, which came to be known as W-M-D, relied on a system of compulsory health insurance and replaced the federal grants in Wagner's original bill with payroll taxes. The plan provided workers and their families with no-cost health care

Senator Robert F. Wagner tried for years to win passage of a bill that would provide health insurance coverage for Americans.

services, including doctors' appointments and visits to the hospital. Unlike the British system, the plan did not provide medical benefits to everyone or set up the government as the owner-operator of the nation's hospitals. The bill also included benefits for people with disabilities; maternity and death benefits; and federal grants to build new hospitals. Opponents of the bill, led by the AMA and their conservative allies in Congress, saw to it that the bill never made it to the floor of Congress for a vote.

President Roosevelt died on April 12, 1945, and Vice President Harry S. Truman took over as president. After guiding the nation to the end of World War II, the new president threw the weight of his office behind national health insurance. Seven months into his presidency, Truman outlined an ambitious plan to improve the quality of U.S. health care and to make it available to every American. He considered it to be government's duty to do everything necessary to see that the people it served had good medical care. Every American, he told Congress, ought to be assured "the right to adequate medical care and the opportunity to achieve and enjoy good health." In November 1945 Truman proposed to:

- Use federal funds to lure doctors to rural areas and other places with few medical providers.
- Provide funding to build new hospitals in areas where needed.
- Establish national standards that all medical centers had to meet.
- Increase federal funding for medical research and education.
- Set up a national health insurance plan, run by the federal government, to cover all Americans.

The last section, which required everyone to enroll in the plan, sparked the most controversy. Under the Truman plan, national health insurance would be an expansion of the Social Security program already in place. Employers and employees would pay for the insurance through payroll deductions and taxes. Government-funded social welfare agencies would foot the bill for poor, unemployed people. Truman intended his insurance plan to cover all Americans—workers and their employers, self-employed business people, professionals, farmers and agricultural laborers, maids and other domestic workers, government employees, the unemployed, and the families of them all. The insurance would cover a broad array of health needs, including medical and dental care, doctors' fees, hospital stays, surgery and other procedures, nursing services, and laboratory tests. The program, Truman said, would guarantee that hospitals and doctors got paid for their work.

A federal approach would provide medical care for all Americans on an equal basis much faster than state-by-state plans could do, the president said. He emphasized that plans would be managed locally, patients would have the freedom to choose their own doctors, and doctors would remain in charge of their practices (either on their own or as part of a group) and decide which treatments to pursue. Americans could buy extra insurance or pay for treatments not offered under the government program. While everyone had to contribute to the plan, doctors could opt not to treat patients covered by the government program. Instead, they could choose to treat only patients who paid for extra services.

Truman reported that 15 million Americans lived in areas without adequate medical facilities. Many more, he said, could not afford to pay for medical care, even where it was available. The rising cost of health care affected not just the poor, but "a large proportion of normally self-supporting persons" as well. The president noted that the United States spent only about 4 percent of the national income on health, including public health agencies and research programs. "We can afford to spend more for health," he declared. He noted that only 3 to 4 percent of Americans carried insurance that covered comprehensive health care. A national compulsory insurance program, he said, would spread the costs and help prevent as well as treat disease.

The president met expected AMA opposition head on. "What I am recommending is not socialized medicine," he said. "Socialized medicine means that all doctors work as employees of government. . . . No such system is here proposed." He concluded his discussion of the insurance plan with a persuasive pitch for support. "We are a rich nation and can afford many things. But ill-health which can be prevented or cured is one thing we cannot afford."

Truman's proposals received little coverage in the nation's media. Newspapers and radio stations carried only a brief mention of them. Television was in its infancy—only five thousand American homes had TV sets at the end of World War II in 1945. Of those who knew about the proposal, however, 59 percent favored it, a Gallup poll revealed. Many Americans learned about the proposals through pamphlets at their doctors' offices or from the many ads placed in newspapers, magazines, and other media by opponents.

With the new session of Congress, Senators Wagner, Murray, and Dingell revised their W-M-D bill to encompass most of Truman's proposals. The bill called for taxes from the general fund to supplement payroll taxes but covered the medical needs of workers and their families only. Many hoped that the national push to increase employment would extend health benefits to almost everyone.

A separate bill, the Hill-Burton Hospital Construction Bill, set up federal grants to states to build hospitals and clinics. Senator Lister Hill, a Democrat from Alabama, and Senator Harold H. Burton, a Republican from Ohio, introduced the bill. Although hospitals benefiting from the bill had to provide some medical services for poor people, the bill did little to address the problem of full treatment for everyone who could not afford to pay for it. It did, however, fund hospitals in regions throughout the country that had been without medical facilities, particularly in the South. Supported by the AHA and the AMA, the Hill-Burton bill passed Congress and was enacted in 1946. The law won approval with little controversy even though it allowed hospitals in the South to segregate white and black patients and essentially to bar African American doctors from hospitals serving white clientele in the South.

FIRESTORM OF CONTROVERSY

The new W-M-D bill, on the other hand, set off a firestorm of controversy. Supporters formed a coalition group, the Committee for the Nation's Health, to educate the public about the bill and lobby for its passage. Members included a wide range of health reformers: labor unions including the national labor associations, Senator Wagner and other leading Democrats, and former First Lady Eleanor Roosevelt. The AMA took the lead in opposing the measure. The doctors' organization waged the most expensive lobbying campaign ever undertaken in America at that time, spending $1.5 million to defeat the bill.

Even though the United States and the Soviet Union had fought as allies against Germany in World War II, the two nations had developed a deep distrust of one another. The Soviet Union, made up of Russia and surrounding Balkan and Eastern European nations, embraced communism, a system where the government owned businesses and party officials supervised operations. The United States, on the other hand, based its system of government on capitalism, which championed private ownership and management. As the Soviet Union grew stronger and wielded more influence, it challenged the position of the United States in the world. After World War II, the two nations became embroiled in a struggle for supremacy. This conflict became known as the cold war (because it involved no actual combat).

The AMA and other opponents of the W-M-D bill used

President Harry S. Truman supported a plan that would have provided health insurance coverage for all Americans.

Americans' fear of the Soviet threat to discredit Truman's health care proposals. They accused everyone connected to the plan of being "red" or "socialist," terms linked to the Soviet Union and communism. Administration members who promoted the plan were branded as "followers of the Moscow party line." The proposals became stuck with the label "socialized medicine" (a system marked by government ownership and operation), even though the plan depended on private health insurers and private doctors and health care providers. Calling it "socialized" made the plan suspect in the eyes of many Americans. They ignored the fact that the proposals were based on the system used by America's strongest ally, Great Britain, a capitalistic nation and one of the world's leading democracies. The New York public relations firm hired by the AMA circulated one pamphlet on the bill that suggested that "socialized medicine" would lead to a socialist takeover of other aspects of life.

A BITTER DISAPPOINTMENT

Although presidents cannot directly submit legislation to Congress or vote on bills, they can play a vital role in winning approval for their proposals. Many take their case to the bargaining table, agreeing to certain changes in their proposals or offering support for a pet project in return for a Congress member's vote. Presidents also use their position as head of their political party—and promises of support during the next campaign—to persuade reluctant members to vote a particular way. If those measures do not work, a president whose party does not control Congress may still influence members by enlisting support from the voters—a great outpouring of citizens in support of a bill may well change the mind (and vote) of a senator or representative.

In Truman's case, neither strategy worked. Powerful conservative Southern Democrats controlled many of the committees in Congress during Truman's first year in office and would not allow the bill to be released for debate. After the 1946 elections, Republicans, who opposed the bill, attained a majority in Congress and took over as committee chairs. The legislation remained tied up in committee during the entire Truman presidency.

In May 1947 Truman conducted a special ceremony to spotlight the health insurance program after visiting his ill mother. The strategy won front-page coverage in the *New York Times*, but it attracted no converts in Congress, which continued to hold the bill in committee.

During the 1948 presidential campaign, Truman continued to push for national health insurance and dismiss AMA's "socialist" label. "Is it un-American to visit the sick, aid the afflicted, or comfort the dying?" he asked voters gathered during a campaign stop. "Does cancer care about political parties? Does infantile paralysis concern itself with income? Of course it doesn't."

Truman's opponent in the presidential race, New York Republican governor Thomas Dewey, came out strongly against the insurance plan. Backed by the AMA, the Chamber of Commerce, and other business interests, Dewey was expected to sweep the election. To everyone's surprise, Truman narrowly defeated Dewey and by January 1949 had won high marks for his performance as president from 69 percent of those polled by Gallup.

Truman continued his pitch for the plan, while the AMA ramped up its campaign to discredit the latest W-M-D bill. Its brochures and public announcements hammered home four points: 1) the United States had the best system of medical care in the world; 2) a government insurance plan would undermine that system and interfere with free enterprise; 3) a government-run system would cost too much; and 4) private insurance already provided adequately for Americans' health care needs.

Truman gave national health insurance a prominent spot in his State of the Union address in 1949. At the same time, though, labor leaders had begun to push employers to provide workers with private health insurance plans instead of devoting their energies to the W-M-D bill, which seemed hopelessly bogged down in committee.

By the end of 1949 the multimillion-dollar AMA campaign was showing impressive results. More than 1,800 groups had endorsed the AMA position on the health insurance issue. These included the AHA, the American Legion, the Chamber of Commerce, the American Dental Association, and the Catholic Church, which had until that time supported the government plan. A *Fortune* magazine poll in 1942 had showed

74 percent of Americans favored the revised W-M-D plan. But a Gallup poll conducted in late 1949 revealed that support for Truman's national health insurance plan had dropped to 51 percent. The following year approval had slipped to 24 percent, while 51 percent said they opposed national health insurance. Meanwhile, the percentage of Americans covered by some form of voluntary health insurance plan had jumped from about 25 percent in 1946 to around 50 percent by 1950.

The AMA's campaign and the popular press's opposition helped turn Congress and the public against the bill. Neither the House nor the Senate voted on the bill during Truman's administration. The American people supported the idea of national health insurance at the end of World War II, but as the economy improved, many no longer saw the need for a government-subsidized program.

In Congress, supporters of national health insurance introduced a version of W-M-D every session for fourteen years, from 1943 to 1957. After Representative Dingell died in 1955, his son, John Dingell Jr., filled his seat in Congress and continued the push for national health insurance. Truman, who championed the cause, left office without any progress toward national health insurance. "I have had some bitter disappointments as President," he wrote in his memoirs, "but the one that has troubled me most, in a personal way, has been the failure to defeat the organized opposition to a national compulsory health-insurance program."

EISENHOWER'S VOLUNTARY PLAN

In the 1950s medical costs continued to climb, but Congress made no progress in developing a plan to help Americans pay for health care. With the national insurance plan pretty much dead, some advocates explored the idea of extending Social Security benefits to include a medical insurance plan that would cover Americans sixty-five or older. Senators Murray and Hubert H. Humphrey of Minnesota and Representatives Dingell and Emanuel Celler of New York, all Democrats, introduced identical bills in 1952 to provide federal health insurance to those who received Social Security. Like the perennial W-M-D, the bill went nowhere.

Republican Dwight D. Eisenhower assumed the presidency in January 1953. During his time in office, the nation's elderly faced a crisis in medical care. In 1950, 12 million Americans were sixty-five or older. Two-thirds of them had annual incomes of less than $1,000; seven in eight had no health insurance of any kind. Yet the elderly population was most at risk for debilitating medical conditions and expensive medications and treatment. Few retired people received health insurance from their former employers.

Medical researchers had made some progress in treating tuberculosis, heart disease, and cancer, and in developing a vaccine against polio, but in 1950 the nation lacked clinics and hospitals to provide advanced treatments. Most Americans, especially those living in rural areas, still depended on the family doctor for their health care needs. People who could not afford to pay for treatment were often reluctant to seek any help at all. "I suppose I could have a doctor come for my husband's sickness, but he won't have it," one woman said. "He gets more crippled all the time, but we just get along financially now, and we haven't any money to pay [the doctor]. We never took any charity, and we're too old to begin to now."

In an address to Congress on the nation's health delivered in January 1954, President Eisenhower acknowledged the difficulties faced by Americans in need of medical care. "Many of our fellow Americans cannot afford to pay the costs of medical care when it is needed, and they are not protected by adequate health insurance," he told Congress and the nation. He also noted that some hospitals lacked the equipment and technology needed to treat disease adequately. The nation suffered from a shortage of trained medical personnel as well, Eisenhower said.

To address these needs, he called for the establishment of a new cabinet-level Department of Health, Education, and Welfare to focus on health issues. In addition, Eisenhower proposed more funding for the National Institutes of Health and other health-oriented research programs, stronger public health programs, and construction of new hospitals. The centerpiece of Eisenhower's plan was based on what he called reinsurance, a system to increase the number of Americans covered by private insurance. Eisenhower firmly rejected any health care program that included compulsory health insurance or government-subsidized insurance plans.

Instead, the Eisenhower proposal would set up a government fund to encourage private insurance companies to offer coverage to a broad range of customers. The companies would buy "reinsurance" from the government to cover higher-risk clients. The government fund would pay private companies with reinsurance up to 75 percent of any losses over the amount of the premiums they collected. Eisenhower estimated the fund would require $25 million, which would then be repaid by the fees from reinsurance.

With high-risk policies partially funded by the government, companies could sell health insurance to many more Americans. By spreading out the cost of insurance over a much wider base, companies could offer coverage at prices most

Americans would be able to afford to pay. Insurance policies could also offer more coverage—for catastrophic illnesses or long hospital stays. Such plans would increase coverage in rural areas and help pay for doctors' visits and home care as well as treatment in hospitals. Health insurance would be voluntary, but because of the lower costs, Eisenhower reasoned, most Americans would sign up for a plan. The president also offered a small increase in federal grants to help states pay medical costs for those who received public assistance already—blind people, dependent children, people with disabilities, and elderly Americans living in poverty.

Eisenhower's plan would require "no Government subsidy and no Government competition with private insurance carriers," the president said. Nonetheless, its critics marshaled enough opposition to defeat the proposal. The AMA in particular campaigned against the plan, which doctors feared would give insurance companies and the government power to limit their income. The president of the AMA warned against the continuing "socialistic trend and government intrusion into business and affairs of the people." The House of Representatives approved Eisenhower's reinsurance program in 1954, but the Senate took no action on the matter and the bill died. Proponents of the plan reintroduced it several more times, but they never succeeded in enacting it.

SUBSIDIES, LOANS, AND HELP FOR RETIREES

Both Republicans and Democrats tried to expand health care coverage in the 1950s. One bill called for subsidized state-managed plans provided by private insurers. Another proposed an early form of managed care, a system in which patients choose from a list of approved health providers, and health care services are controlled to increase efficiency and reduce costs. None of the bills passed. Nevertheless, the fight for medical benefits made several gains during the Eisenhower years. In 1956 Congress set up a health insurance program, managed and funded by the federal government, for family members of military personnel. That same year Congress increased payments for medical care for poor Americans being served by welfare programs. Congress also ordered a study on the medical issues faced by elderly Americans. This, in turn, would bolster the campaign to provide health care for older citizens.

In 1957 the AFL-CIO—the national labor group formed as a result of the merger between the American Federation of Labor and the Congress for Industrial Organization—threw its weight behind an effort to provide medical insurance for retirees. Representative Aime J. Forand, a Democrat from Rhode Island, introduced the labor-backed bill in the House in 1958. It, too, failed in the wake of AMA attacks, even though the AHA asked Congress to hold hearings on the various bills. The nation's hospitals had long borne the burden of providing care for elderly patients unable to pay for such services. As the elderly population increased, this burden threatened the financial stability of some hospitals, and they hoped a government-financed health plan for elderly Americans would help ease their budget problems.

CHAPTER THREE

Passage of Medicare

Members of both parties felt pressured to do something about the nation's increasingly expensive health care system and the number of Americans who received little or no medical treatment. Democrats supported compulsory health insurance, while their counterparts in the Republican Party promoted a voluntary insurance plan. Conservative Republicans and their allies, the southern Democrats, favored a hands-off approach, preferring instead to leave private interests to deal with the problem. They feared a government takeover of the nation's health care system and also were concerned that providing universal benefits would bankrupt the country.

In 1960 Representative Aime J. Forand reintroduced his insurance bill for retired Americans. After Eisenhower's new secretary of Health, Education, and Welfare, Arthur Flemming, told Congress that the administration still opposed compulsory insurance plans, the AFL-CIO organized older

Americans in rallies across the country in support of the bill. Six thousand elderly citizens in Manhattan booed at the mention of Eisenhower and cheered when one speaker said, "We've got a President who has spent his entire life on the public payroll. He has never paid a doctor's bill, and he is still saying there is no need for a Forand bill." Despite this show of support, the bill languished in committee. Similar bills introduced by Senators Hubert H. Humphrey and John F. Kennedy did not cover surgical procedures but still failed to produce the votes needed for passage.

In the waning days of his presidency, Eisenhower proposed a voluntary health insurance plan that covered 80 percent of the cost of hospitalization (up to 180 days), surgery, rehabilitation and nursing services, care in a nursing home, doctors' and dentists' fees, and up to $350 worth of prescription drugs. Those who qualified and chose to enroll would pay a monthly premium of twenty-four dollars. The problem with the proposal, however, was that it was up to the states to decide whether to participate in the program. States that adopted the plan would determine who could enroll and set the terms and benefits actually paid. At best, it promised an uneven benefits package for poor Americans, with good coverage for a large number of lower-income citizens in some states and health care for only a few of the neediest people in other states.

House Ways and Means chairman Wilbur Mills of Arkansas pushed through a watered-down version of the Eisenhower bill. With fellow-Democrat Robert Kerr from Oklahoma, Mills introduced legislation that provided federal money for health insurance for poor elderly Americans. The program was completely voluntary, with grants going to states that chose to provide such coverage and that could match the federal funds. With Forand's bill and similar proposals still stalled in committee, Mills's bill passed with little fanfare and became law in August 1960. Two years later, fewer than half the states had applied for federal money under the law. The legislation would later form the basis of the Medicaid program for poor elderly Americans.

During the 1960 presidential campaign, the platforms of both parties advocated some kind of help for Americans in attaining health care. Democrats pledged to support the right of Americans "to adequate medical care and the opportunity to achieve and enjoy good health." Noting the plight of the nation's poor elderly citizens, the Democratic platform supported the extension of the Social Security program to cover hospital bills and costly medical services for older Americans. Democratic nominee John F. Kennedy's approach focused on creating more jobs and encouraging employers to provide health insurance for more workers and retirees.

On the Republican side, the platform pledged to support programs to protect elderly Americans against the "burdensome costs of health care." The Republican presidential candidate, Richard M. Nixon, was an advocate for more jobs for retirees who wanted to keep working, additional federal money for medical research and hospitals, and government subsidies to help older people buy private health insurance.

KENNEDY'S PLAN FOR RETIREES

After winning a tight race, Kennedy announced his support in February 1961 for a plan that would expand Social Security to provide retired Americans with basic coverage for hospital treatment as well as outpatient care. Kennedy's advisers fashioned a moderate plan, focused only on older Americans, that they believed would pass. Democrats in Congress

Operation Coffee Cup

As part of its blitz against the King-Anderson bill, the AMA hired actor Ronald Reagan to be the spokesman in a national public relations campaign called Operation Coffee Cup. Reagan recorded a speech that portrayed the bill as the first step in a plan to convert America into a socialist country.

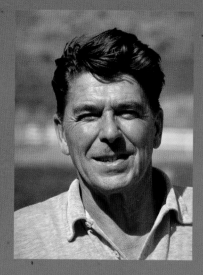

Ronald Reagan in 1965

The actor's polished, calm delivery, which later helped him win the presidency, persuaded listeners to support the AMA's case against the bill, an earlier version of Medicare. The ten-minute recording went to doctors' wives across the nation. These members of the AMA's Women's Auxiliary played the recording for friends and neighbors at coffee get-togethers at their homes. Operating under AMA guidelines, the auxiliary instructed listeners to write personal messages opposing the bill so members of Congress would think the letters were from ordinary voters and not part of an organized campaign.

In the recording, Reagan characterized the insurance plan as "socialized medicine" and said the bill was just a "foot in the door" for socialists to take over America. Under the plan advocated in the King-Anderson bill, the government would dictate how many patients doctors could see, where doctors should locate their practice, and what kind of medicine they could pursue, Reagan said. If the women listening to his voice did not take action against the legislation, Reagan warned, "One of these days you and I are going to spend our sunset years telling our children, and our children's children, what it once was like in America when we were free."

incorporated the president's plan as the King-Anderson bill, named after its sponsors, Representative Cecil King of California and Senator Clinton P. Anderson of New Mexico. To head off AMA criticism, regular doctors' fees were omitted from the plan. Even so, the AMA and the AHA opposed the legislation, as did chairman Mills. The House Ways and Means Committee, under Mills's control, blocked the bill from ever reaching the House floor for debate.

The following year, Kennedy repeated his pitch to include hospital insurance for older Americans under Social Security. The program, he said, "would not interfere in any way with the freedom of choice of doctor, hospital, or nurse." Despite that reassurance, the second proposal went the way of the first. With the plan in trouble, Kennedy backed off from a full-scale battle for the proposal because he feared antagonizing powerful conservative members of Congress, whose votes he needed to pass a tax bill and trade legislation. A threatened missile attack by Cuba and other extremely pressing matters in foreign affairs kept the president from launching a more aggressive campaign for the health insurance bill.

After President Kennedy was assassinated in November 1963, Vice President Lyndon B. Johnson assumed the presidency and took up the fight for health insurance for older Americans. Opponents of Johnson's proposal pushed for a bill that would increase monthly payments under Social Security but would not include health insurance. By doing so, they hoped to use up funds that could otherwise go toward health insurance. They also wanted to appease older voters, who voiced considerable support for the added insurance benefit. The president succeeded in persuading the Senate to oppose the alternate measure, but Mills used his power to hold the president's insurance plan in committee again.

LBJ'S ALL-OUT CAMPAIGN FOR HEALTH BENEFITS
Voters returned Johnson to office in 1964 and elected a huge
Democratic majority in both houses of Congress. The president, a master politician, used that advantage in his effort to
provide retirees with health insurance. One of his first acts
was to recruit Wilbur Mills, a fellow southern Democrat, to
put together a workable plan that insured retirees' health
costs. The resulting plan, which amended the Social Security
Act, became known as Medicare.

During the process, older Americans and their supporters
launched an all-out campaign to push for health benefits.
Former Representative Forand set up the National Council of Senior Citizens for Medical Care in 1961 to lobby for
health benefits for older Americans. With support from the
AFL-CIO and the Democratic National Committee, the organization became a national force, holding rallies throughout
the country. Other groups, such as the Golden Ring Council, a
group representing New York's older citizens, joined the fray.

Senior citizens picketed state AMA offices, signed peti-
tions, wrote letters to members of Congress, distributed flyers, polled doctors, sponsored debates, and collected money
for advertising to promote the legislation. With 17 million
older Americans, senior citizens represented a powerful
lobby. Although Americans of retirement age represented
less than 10 percent of the population (186.5 million at the
time), they made up almost 15 percent of citizens who voted
regularly in 1964. That percentage continued to grow during
the following decades as seniors became active lobbyists for
causes that affected them.

In January 1964 hundreds of "energetic, elderly persons"
turned out to support medical care for older Americans at a
hearing in New York City. "The need [for medical care cover-

Older Americans picket at the Democratic National Convention in 1964 in support of President Johnson's Medicare program.

age] is dire," one seventy-two-year-old woman said. For the first time in the decades-long battle for health insurance, a group of Americans made enough noise and conducted large enough protests to gain the full attention of Congress.

Both the AHA and insurance companies saw the need for government help in paying for medical care for elderly Americans. Because of an increased risk of health problems, older citizens had higher medical bills, which hospitals often had to cover and which left private insurers with little or no profit on their policies.

The AMA continued to oppose the legislation. To forestall what the medical society termed "socialized medicine," the AMA proposed a plan of its own called Eldercare. The voluntary insurance plan expanded insurance benefits to cover both doctors' fees and hospital costs and offered a sliding scale based on income.

Members of the Johnson administration, Mills, and other

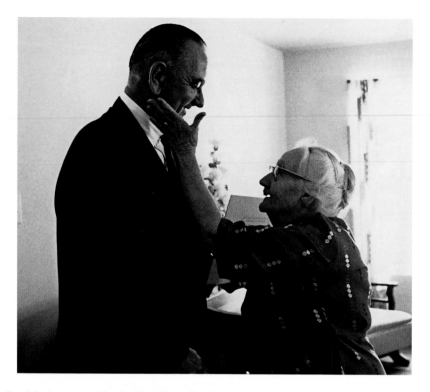

An elderly woman thanks President Lyndon B. Johnson for his support of the Medicare health care bill in April 1965.

congressional leaders hammered out a three-part program that combined the Democrats' compulsory health insurance, the Republicans' voluntary plan, and the charity-based program favored by conservatives. The revised King-Anderson bill, with federally funded health insurance providing coverage for hospital treatment for all retirees, became Part A of the Medicare bill. Part B incorporated the AMA's Eldercare proposal and provided a voluntary insurance program, subsidized by the government, to cover doctors' fees. Medicaid, based on the Kerr-Mills law, formed the third tier of the proposal. It set up a state-run program to provide medical care for poor Americans, financed with federal and state money.

Dubbed the "three-layer cake," the Medicare bill offered compromises to meet opponents' objections. Even with these concessions, the AMA mounted another national campaign to defeat the Medicare/Medicaid bill. This time, however, the playing field had shifted. A growing number of doctors privately conceded they supported Medicare, or at least did not oppose it. A group of New York senior citizens, under the banner of the Golden Ring Council, polled their doctors on the Kennedy health benefits package in 1962. The results showed that 85 percent of the 1,500 doctors polled favored the bill, but many said they were afraid to take a public stand against the AMA's official position in the matter. In addition, older Americans overwhelmingly demonstrated their support for the bill. Its backers made the political compromises necessary to smooth the bill's passage, and President Johnson used his power to push the law through Congress.

On July 27 the House of Representatives voted 307 to 116 to enact the measure. The Senate followed suit, approving the bill on a 70 to 24 vote on July 28. On July 30, 1965, with former President Harry S. Truman sitting at his side at the Truman Library and Museum in Independence, Missouri, President Johnson signed the Medicare bill into law. It was the first national bill ever to legislate compulsory health insurance for American citizens. Limited though it was to retirees (later extended to cover people with disabilities), the law was considered a major milestone in the decades-long campaign for universal health insurance coverage. Calling Truman "the real daddy of Medicare," the sitting president credited Truman's Fair Deal with being the inspiration behind the 1965 health benefits program. After signing the bill, Johnson presented the first two Medicare cards to the beaming former president and his wife, Bess.

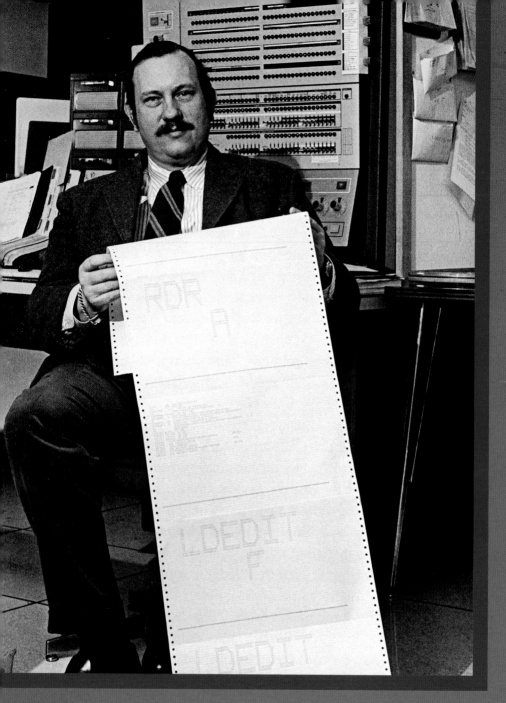

In 1970, Dr. John Knowles, director of Massachusetts General Hospital in Boston, displaying a long computer bill listing all the charges for one patient. He estimated the hospital paid $500,000 a year for the extra paperwork required by insurance companies and government regulators. This led to the Nixon-Kennedy efforts to pass a health-reform act.

CHAPTER FOUR

Nixon and Kennedy Efforts

With the passage of the Medicare bill, proponents of universal health care saw the promise of an even bigger victory that soon would bring health insurance coverage to all Americans. The problems encountered by the Medicare and Medicaid programs, however, dashed those hopes.

While the new law helped older Americans and those with disabilities to pay their medical bills, it did nothing to check the nation's spiraling health care costs. Over the next five years, the cost of medical care increased nearly twice as fast as the cost of living. By 1973 the bill for health care consumed 11 percent of the federal budget, compared to 4 percent in 1965. Part of the reason for the jump was the sudden spike in demand among those enrolled in Medicare. With no accompanying increase in doctors or medical facilities, the increase in demand hiked up prices.

Paperwork required by the system also contributed to the rising costs. Claims had to be processed by the government and insurance companies, adding another layer of bureau-cracy. The government absorbed many of the highest-risk cases, increasing costs even more. The struggle to pay for Medicare convinced Johnson not to seek a similar plan to cover the nation's children.

The increase in medical costs was one factor in the rise of private insurance plans. By 1965 employers provided some form of health insurance for 70 percent of American work-ers. But even those who were covered by insurance faced growing debts for medical care. Elderly Americans who had both Medicare and private insurance found they still had to pay two-thirds of their health bills. Richard Nixon, who suc-ceeded Johnson to the presidency in 1968, ordered wage and price freezes in 1971 to try to control inflation and rein in health care costs. The regulations limited the amount doctors and hospitals could increase their rates. Health pro-viders adopted several other measures, including the expan-sion of programs to manage health care.

Unions rallied behind a generous universal health bene-fits plan developed in 1970 by the Committee for National Health Insurance (CNHI), a private group headed by United Auto Workers president Leonard Woodcock. Under the com-mittee's Health Security Plan, the government would pay for hospital treatment, doctors' care, mental health therapy, dental services, nursing home care, medical equipment, and prescription drugs for all Americans. The program would be financed by payroll taxes and the federal government.

The plan would take the place of health insurance policies and replace the patchwork of overlapping state and federal programs already in existence. Everyone would be required to participate in the program, which would be administered by an independent health security board. Advocates of the

plan estimated it would cost the federal government $6 billion more than the money already spent on existing federal programs, including Medicare. They noted that employers, employees, and others covered by private insurance would no longer have to pay premiums for benefits.

Polls showed that the public backed national health insurance by a two-to-one margin. In 1971 Senator Edward Kennedy, who chaired the Senate's Health Subcommittee and had served on the CNHI, and Representative Martha Griffiths, a Michigan Democrat, included the National Health Insurance Committee's "Health Security Plan" in their bill promoting national health insurance.

President Nixon opposed the government-run program and presented a plan of his own that relied heavily on private insurance companies. Nixon had grown up in a poor family, and two of his brothers died young from tuberculosis. He had seen firsthand the devastating effects of high medical bills on a family's finances and believed in making health care accessible to Americans. While a congressman from California, Nixon sponsored a bill for national health insurance as early as 1947. The president's plan required employers to pay for health insurance for their workers and relied on private insurance companies to provide coverage.

Democrats thought the president's plan did not provide enough benefits. Kennedy charged that the proposal benefited insurance companies too much and workers too little. He called Nixon's plan a "partnership program that will provide billions of dollars to the health insurance companies." One problem with Nixon's plan was that it would cover less than half of subscribers' medical expenses. The Kennedy plan would cover about 70 percent of subscribers' medical bills, but it would also cost an estimated $60 billion to run.

Edward M. Kennedy, brother to a president and a one-time presidential contender, devoted his life to the U.S. Senate, where he spent forty-seven years advocating for liberal causes. A Democrat from Massachusetts, he helped pass laws to end discrimination against people with disabilities, pushed for more money for cancer research and AIDS, and led civil rights and immigration reform efforts.

The campaign to provide affordable health care to every American, however, was, in his words, the "passion of my life." He had witnessed firsthand the devastation caused by ill health. A sister was mentally disabled, and Kennedy himself spent seven months in the hospital after a plane crash that nearly killed him. Two of his children battled cancer. His son Edward M. Kennedy Jr. lost a leg to the disease when he was twelve. Daughter Kara was told she had only a year to live after she developed lung cancer. Kennedy found his daughter another doctor, who successfully treated her.

The senator recalled one of the "searing memories" of his life as he watched over his son, who had to endure experimental treatment for bone cancer. The treatments, administered for three days every three weeks for two years, cost $3,000 for each three-week session. Kennedy's health insurance, provided by the federal government for all members of Congress, paid for the treatment. But other families who had children with the same condition were forced to sell their houses to cover the costs. Even then, some could afford only four months' worth of treatments for their ill children.

"My child was going to have the best because I had the health insurance of the United States Senate," Kennedy said. "No one else had that kind of coverage. That kind of choice for any parent in this country is absolutely unacceptable and wrong. If that health insurance is good enough for the members of the Congress of the United States and good

Passion

At left, a mourner holds a tribute to Edward M. Kennedy as the hearse carrying the senator's body makes a farewell stop at the U.S. Capitol on the way to Arlington National Cemetery on August 29, 2009. Above, Edward M. Kennedy in 2009.

enough for the president, it is good enough for . . . everyone across this country."

For forty years Senator Kennedy supported—and often led—every congressional campaign for national health insurance. He died in August 2009, seven months before Congress passed the Patient Protection and Affordable Care Act, legislation he helped guide through the Senate until brain cancer ended his personal battle against the disease.

President Richard Nixon in 1971. Nixon pushed for a national health insurance program that relied on private insurers.

The AMA floated an alternate plan calling for tax credits to encourage people to buy their own policies. The AHA favored the establishment of nonprofit corporations to administer health insurance plans for employers and poor Americans.

In all, Congress considered fourteen bills on health insurance during the session. A majority in Congress came out in support of the concept. Both parties believed that backing a national health plan would enhance their chances in upcoming elections. Many, including Representative Mills, were convinced that Congress would enact a bill during the session to provide Americans with some form of health coverage. None of the bills, however, won enough support to pass.

The growing health care crisis continued unabated as Congress struggled to deal with the issue. Twenty-five million Americans, most of whom were poor and at high risk for medical problems, carried no health insurance and had little access to medical care. Few policies included coverage for catastrophic illnesses such as heart disease and cancer, which could bankrupt families faced with huge medical bills. Forty percent of those with health insurance had no coverage for doctors' visits, and few plans paid for services designed to prevent illness.

HMOS: COST SAVINGS AND CRITICISM

During the next session, Congress passed the Health Maintenance Act of 1973 in an effort to curb the rising cost of medical care. Sponsored by Senator Kennedy and Representative Paul G. Rogers, a Florida Democrat, the bill provided federal grants and loans to help set up health maintenance organizations, or HMOs, throughout the country. President Nixon signed the measure into law on December 29, 1973. He viewed it as "another milestone" that would complement his overall national health plan.

Under the HMO system, members paid monthly premiums in exchange for medical treatment provided by participating doctors, hospitals, clinics, and other medical professionals and services. In most plans, a member chose a primary care physician within the network, who determined what additional care the patient was entitled to. In order to obtain specialized care, a patient had to get referrals from the primary care doctor, acting under HMO guidelines. HMOs were touted as a more efficient way of managing health care and providing preventive care. Advocates reasoned that HMOs would have a financial incentive to keep members healthy.

The AMA opposed the HMO concept, but the Nixon administration praised the new law as a way to hold down costs and make medical care more accessible to lower- and middle-class Americans. Critics charged that the system put too much emphasis on cost-cutting at the expense of quality care.

"THE CLOSEST WE HAVE EVER COME"

President Nixon presented his revised national insurance plan to Congress the next January. The Comprehensive Health Insurance Plan (CHIP) offered every American health insurance through one of three options: plans provided through a person's work; low-cost programs, subsidized by the government, for people not qualifying for other plans (people paid what they could based on their income and the government paid the rest); or Medicare, which would be expanded to include additional benefits for older Americans. All three programs would be voluntary and would offer identical benefits to participants. The insurance would cover the costs of hospital care, doctors' services, treatment for mental illness, prescription drugs, tests and medical devices, and other health care needs. The plan also provided for home health services as a way to limit long stays in nursing homes. In addition to providing regular medical care for children, the plan provided prevention programs during a child's first six years of life, regular dental care to age thirteen, and eye and hearing exams.

Insurance would be provided by private insurers, under government guidelines. No one could be cut off because of serious illness; the plan banned lifetime caps on benefits. Participants in any of the CHIP plans could obtain medical care across the country. Providers billed the insurance company, which billed policyholders for their share, if any.

Nixon promoted CHIP in a special message to Congress on February 6, 1974. Millions of Americans, he said, either had no health insurance coverage or carried policies that did not fully protect them and their families. "These gaps in health protection can have tragic consequences," Nixon told Congress. "They can cause people to delay seeking medical attention until it is too late. Then a medical crisis ensues, followed by huge medical bills—or worse. Delays in treatment can end in death or lifelong disability."

The president said the plan, which he estimated would cost an additional $5.9 billion a year, could be paid for with existing funds and would not require a tax increase. More doctors, increases in medical school enrollments, and recent cuts in hospital costs, Nixon noted, would help prevent the price hikes that took place after Medicare went into effect. He also proposed several steps to help keep medical costs in check. Under the Nixon proposals, states would have the authority to oversee rates, plans, reimbursements, and other aspects of insurance company operations. Insurers would be required to operate plans effectively and efficiently to control costs. States that did not supervise companies' operations would lose federal funds for health insurance.

Nixon noted that the plan encouraged competition among insurance companies to come up with the best plan for the lowest price. This would be a big factor in cutting costs. By providing insurance for every American who wanted to participate, the national plan offered a huge increase in business to private firms, strengthening private enterprise, he said.

The president urged Congress to pass the legislation as soon as possible. "Comprehensive health insurance is an idea whose time has come in America," he declared. Senator Kennedy said the president's new plan was "a serious and carefully prepared proposal." He submitted a compromise bill, cosponsored by Mills, which expanded the role of private insurers but retained a government-run plan.

The two plans had the same goal of national health coverage for Americans and cost around the same amount to operate, approximately $40 billion. Both proposals called for employers to pay 75 percent of premiums for their workers, with employees paying the remaining 25 percent. Both also covered preventive care and required all but the poorest Americans to pay deductibles up to a certain limit. The plans had some differences, however. The Kennedy–Mills bill set up a government-run program to provide basic health care, while putting private firms in charge of adjusting claims and disbursing funds. Nixon's proposal funneled about $37 million to private insurers, who would manage their own plans. While the president's program required employers to participate but gave employees the option of participating, the Kennedy-Mills bill mandated that both enroll.

Unions continued to back the original government-run, universal health care plan, estimated to cost twice as much as the Nixon or Kennedy plan. That plan would be paid for by corporate and payroll taxes, with no individual contributions.

News reporters discussing the proposals in April 1974 predicted that Congress would pass a health care plan "either late this year but certainly no later than next year." All the pieces seemed to be in place for the adoption of a national health insurance plan.

In May, Nixon offered to compromise on parts of his plan in an effort to win passage of a national health care bill. Kennedy initially agreed to work with the president on a new plan. Meeting secretly, Kennedy and Nixon each made concessions to develop a new proposal. Both encountered opposition from factions that usually supported them. The AMA, insurance companies, and conservatives pressured Nixon to oppose Kennedy's "socialized medicine" plan. Labor leaders urged Kennedy to back their proposal. Rather than agreeing to concessions, labor unions chose to wait for a shift in power, believing a Democratic president would offer a better deal for workers. Labor's opposition became so vehement that Kennedy eventually backed away from the compromise.

Nixon, too, abandoned the efforts at compromise—but not willingly. For months pressure had been building in Congress to impeach the president for his role in the Watergate scandal that linked Nixon and his closest aides to a break-in at the Democratic national headquarters during the campaign for the presidency in 1972 and the subsequent effort to cover up their involvement in the affair. On July 24, the U.S. Supreme Court ordered Nixon to release secret tapes of White House meetings and conversations. Three days later, the House Judiciary Committee charged Nixon with obstruction of justice and passed the first of three articles of impeachment. Disgraced and under pressure from former allies to resign, Nixon announced his decision to step down from the presidency. On August 9, 1974, Gerald Ford became the nation's thirty-eighth president.

With Nixon out of office, President Ford was left with a disillusioned nation and an unresolved health bill. The new president appealed to Congress to approve a national health plan and ranked the issue second only in importance to inflation on the domestic agenda. Representative Mills continued the effort to forge a compromise. His committee approved a modified version of the Kennedy-Mills bill by a narrow, one-vote margin. In August, he shelved the legislation until he could build a larger majority for the plan. Before he could do that,

Representative Wilbur Mills, chairman of the powerful House Ways and Means Committee, lost his position after a sex scandal in 1974. As a result he never reintroduced the Democrats' health insurance plan in Congress.

however, Mills himself became embroiled in a scandal when police caught him driving drunk with a stripper in his car. Although Mills retained his seat in Congress during elections in November, Democrats removed him from his powerful post as chairman of the House Ways and Means Committee.

Kennedy later acknowledged that Democrats should have worked harder for a compromise plan in 1974. Health care policy expert Paul Starr echoed that view. "In retrospect, 1974 was the closest we have ever come to enacting national health insurance," Starr said in 2009. "Democrats made a great mistake by not eagerly embracing Nixon's proposal. The distance between Kennedy and Nixon then was so small by comparison with the distance that exists now between Democrats and Republicans." The demise of the compromise effort in 1974 derailed any chance of national health insurance under a Ford administration.

CHAPTER FIVE

The Clinton Initiative

The presidential campaign of 1976 demonstrated conclusively that former President Richard M. Nixon's version of national health insurance was dead. Democrats and Republicans both mentioned affordable health care during their conventions, but no other resemblance to the Nixon plan could be found in either party platform. The Republicans made a pitch for "quality health care at an affordable price," but they avoided backing any specific plan. Instead, they promoted the idea of allowing each state to manage its own health programs—the opposite of the approach Nixon had taken. Democrats supported a government-financed plan that, unlike Nixon's voluntary system, required every American to participate.

Democrat Jimmy Carter, who defeated President Gerald Ford in November, proposed a national health insurance plan as a way to deal with the harmful effects of out-of-control medical costs on the ailing economy. His plan covered the cost of major illnesses for most Americans and expanded coverage under Medicare and Medicaid. Senator Edward Kennedy supported a more comprehensive plan that also provided basic medical treatment. Kennedy, who ran against Carter for the party's nomination in 1980, eventually withdrew support for a compromise plan that he said did not cover preventive medicine and provided little help to struggling Americans. Carter later blamed Kennedy for the defeat of health care reform under his administration. Economic concerns, including high inflation and unemployment, played into Congress's failure to act on the proposals.

When Ronald Reagan unseated Carter as president in 1980, he clung to the views he had championed as a spokesman for the American Medical Association—that health care should not be the responsibility of the federal government. He did, however, sign an extension of the Medicare program to provide catastrophic illness coverage for older Americans. The bill limited the amount Medicare recipients had to pay for approved medical treatment to $2,000 a year. Congress enacted the Medicare Catastrophic Illness Coverage Act in 1988 but repealed it a year later after older Americans refused to pay the extra premiums required by the plan.

In 1986 Congress passed the Emergency Medical Treatment and Active Labor Act. Nicknamed the "Patient Anti-Dumping Act," the law barred hospitals from turning away people who were in danger of dying or mothers about to give birth. The law had no provisions, however, for reimbursing hospitals for unpaid services or for coverage for people who needed tests, treatment, or medications to survive.

By the 1990s, health care had once again become front-page news. Some 37 million Americans of a total population of 248.7 million (almost 15 percent) had moved into the

Members of the National Council of Senior Citizens demand that President Reagan address the health care crisis during a Philadelphia rally in 1984.

ranks of the uninsured. Tens of millions more had policies that offered only minimal coverage. Businesses had joined in the chorus of voices demanding that the problem be addressed. In response to a survey conducted by the Robert Wood Johnson Foundation in 1991, a majority of the executives questioned said the health care system could not be fixed without government intervention, though 66 percent opposed a government-run plan. In November 1991 Harris

Wofford based his campaign on the right of every American to health care and became the first Pennsylvania Democrat in thirty years to win election to the U.S. Senate.

Two months later, Democratic presidential candidate Bill Clinton made it clear that health care reform would play a central role in his campaign. "All of our efforts to strengthen the economy will fail unless we take bold steps to reform our health care system," he told supporters. "The American people expect us to deal with health care. And we must deal with it now." After winning the nod to be his party's nominee in the upcoming presidential race, Clinton pledged to "take on the health care profiteers and make health care afford-able for every family." Half of Americans said the nation's health care system was broken, and 40 percent said it needed a complete overhaul, according to a poll conducted in September 1991 by the *New York Times* and CBS News.

Clinton won the presidency and embraced health care as one of his top priorities. On January 25, 1993, five days after taking office, he announced the creation of a task force on national health reform. The president named First Lady Hill-ary Clinton to head the task force with the assignment of preparing a health care reform bill within one hundred days, an extraordinarily difficult undertaking given the complexity of the issue. The bill, it was understood, would set up a sys-tem to provide health insurance coverage for all Americans.

Over the next few months, the task force tweaked doz-ens of proposals to come up with a plan both Democrats and Republicans would support. When it disbanded in May after the allotted one hundred days, the task force had pro-duced a bare-bones structure of a new system but no specific proposal. The White House's health policy team took over the task of developing a plan to bring to Congress.

Big Bucks from Health Care

The health care industry made dramatic gains in profits, executive salaries, and the value of stock in the 1990s. In 1996 *Fortune* magazine included twelve health care companies in its annual list of the country's one hundred fastest-growing firms. One health care company, Oxford Health Plans, posted profits that increased at a compound rate of 75 percent during the decade. From 1991 to 1997 the company's stocks rose from $4 a share to $89 a share. In the late 1990s, Oxford stock fell as the company lost money, but it rebounded at the end of 1999.

Executive salaries at both profit and nonprofit health care companies soared as well. A *New York Times* article in 1992 reported that the nation's largest nonprofit hospitals paid their top executives between $500,000 and $700,000 a year, while the president of New York Hospital-Cornell Medical Center received $860,684 in salary and benefits in 1990.

That trend continued into the twenty-first century. *Forbes* magazine reported in 2005 that United Health Group paid its CEO a package worth $124.8 million in annual salary, stocks, and other benefits. An article in *Vanity Fair* in 2009 reported that chief executive officers at health-care companies are "the highest paid of any industry." On the average, they made more than $12.4 million a year, two-thirds more than CEOs at financial firms.

By 2009, according to the article, the total annual profit of health care firms had reached an estimated $200 billion. In 2010, in the midst of a downturn in the economy, health care executives continued to take home pay packages worth millions. At the top of the list was Medco Health's CEO, who received $25 million in yearly compensation.

By early summer, the team had produced the first draft of a detailed health plan. It relied on managed care to control costs and promote efficient operations and included regional health alliances that would negotiate with private insurers for the best rates. The plan put caps on insurance premiums and required employers to pay for workers' health insurance.

OPPONENTS TAKE AIM

Clinton decided to deal with health care as soon as the budget bill passed. He expected quick passage, but the budget won approval only after a seven-month struggle and the vote of Vice President Al Gore to break a tie in the Senate.

Critics began to marshal forces against the plan even before it was presented. Opponents raised concerns over the cost of the Clinton plan, noting that Medicare and Medicaid expenses had skyrocketed. They objected to the creation of a new government bureaucracy, which they feared would set arbitrary price controls that would drive some doctors and hospitals out of business. They worried that the plan might also undercut employers' insurance programs already in place and encourage millions of Americans who had coverage to join government-funded programs instead.

The Health Insurance Association of America (HIAA), which represented more than three hundred of the nation's health insurance companies, launched a $3.5 million advertising campaign to promote its views and conduct market research on the public's response to the issue. The National Federation of Independent Business (NFIB), lobbyists for small-business owners, began its own campaign against the upcoming bill. NFIB mailings to members and other lobbying efforts targeted a provision that would require employers to provide health insurance for their workers.

In early September the HIAA introduced Harry and Louise to Americans. The couple, portrayed by actors, discussed their concerns about the health care bill and immediately roused fears in the public, who until then had been told little about the details of the proposal. Though the ad's Harry and Louise were not real people, the public identified with them. By the end of the battle, the HIAA had spent $50 million on the ad campaign and a massive grassroots operation that contacted members of Congress more than 450,000 times.

Hillary Clinton lambasted the ads for distorting the plan. On November 1, in a speech at the American Academy of Pediatrics, she accused HIAA of "great lies" and the insurance industry of bringing the nation "to the brink of bankruptcy" with its greed.

HEALTH CARE THAT IS ALWAYS THERE

Under the Clinton plan, Americans could choose from a number of health plans offered by insurance companies, but most people would presumably select managed care plans with lower premiums. Regional health alliances—large groups of consumers—would buy health care services from networks of doctors, hospitals, and other medical professionals. Competition among networks would serve to keep costs down.

The plan provided all Americans with comprehensive medical and dental care, paid for prescription drugs and at-home care for older Americans and those with disabilities, limited yearly medical costs for families to $3,000, and transferred coverage when workers left one job for another. It also put limits on how much insurance companies could raise their rates. To promote quality of care, the plan required insurers to submit reports on treatments and results. The Clinton proposal required everyone to be enrolled in a health

Meet Harry and Louise

A white middle-class couple named Harry and Louise worried aloud about how the Clinton health insurance plan would affect them in ads that ran on national TV in 1993 and 1994. Designed to turn middle America against the Clinton plan, the ads opened with the fictional couple sorting through bills scattered atop their kitchen table in suburbia. "Having choices we don't like is no choice at all," said Louise, portrayed by professional actor Louise Caire Clark. Actor Harry Johnson, in the role of Harry, crumpled a piece of paper in obvious frustration over the government health plan options. The ad ended with the couple's catchiest line, which cleverly positioned the government ("they") against the American people ("we"): "If they choose, we lose."

The couple starred in more than a dozen Harry and Louise ads during the campaign. The Health Insurance Association of America footed the bill for the ads, estimated to cost $14 million. Political commentators credited the ads with raising fears about the Clinton plan and contributing to its demise.

In 2008 the couple made a surprising comeback to urge candidates for president to put health care at the top of their agenda. "Bring everyone to the table and make it happen," Louise said in a reversal of her character's previous stand. The new ads were financed by a coalition of groups favoring affordable health care for Americans and two organizations that had opposed national health insurance in the past—the American Hospital Association and the National Federation of Independent Business.

After the introduction of President Obama's health insurance plan in 2009, the couple continued their pitch for national insurance. In the new ads, Harry triumphantly announced, "It looks like we may finally get health care reform." Louise mused, "A little more cooperation, a little less politics, and we can get the job done this time."

President Bill Clinton delivers his long-awaited presentation of the health care plan on September 22, 1993, in a televised address to Americans.

insurance plan, either through an employer or on their own. All but the poorest Americans paid a portion of the cost of coverage, which was subsidized by the government.

The administration estimated the government's subsidies would cost about $90 billion a year. That would be offset by cost-cutting measures, greater efficiency, and new taxes on cigarettes. Cost cutting and efficiency measures in Medicare and Medicaid would also save money.

On September 22 President Clinton, in a televised address to Congress and the nation, outlined the long-awaited plan. "At long last, after decades of false starts, we must make this our most urgent priority: giving every American health security, health care that can never be taken away, health care

First Lady Hillary Clinton testified before Congress in the fall of 1993 on the health care plan she helped develop.

that is always there. That is what we must do tonight," the president said.

The speech drew repeated applause from Congress and general agreement on the need for health care reform. "It's a great start on a long, tough journey," Senator James M. Jeffords, a moderate Vermont Republican, told the *New York Times*. "He'll get the public on our backs to get the job done."

The following week, Hillary Clinton appeared before five congressional committees to give testimony on the health proposals produced by her team. The plan was still being revised and had not yet been submitted to Congress as a bill. "It is a bizarre situation," she said, "to have a country in which there is parent after parent . . . who had to give up a job [and go on welfare] to take care of their children's medical needs."

President Clinton devoted much of October persuading reluctant Democrats to vote for the North American Free Trade Agreement (NAFTA). By the end of October, when Clinton addressed Congress on the revised Health Security Act, the momentum for the plan had dwindled.

BILL INTRODUCED IN CONGRESS

The Clinton bill, dubbed the Health Security Act, was finally introduced by Majority Leader Richard A. Gephardt of Missouri in the House and by Majority Leader George J. Mitchell of Maine in the Senate, on November 20, just before the session ended. Gephardt predicted Congress would pass the bill in 1994 and "do away—forever—with the anxiety that too many Americans feel today about their health insurance: that it will cost more than they can afford; that they can't get coverage or will lose it; that it won't cover what they need."

Businesses objected that buying workers' health insurance—even through alliances—would cost too much. Brewing company Anheuser-Busch distributed cards advising Budweiser drinkers to call 1-800-BEER-TAX. Those who did heard the firm's claim that a national health insurance plan could result in higher beer taxes. Other firms, however, applauded the plan. Ford and Apple, which both paid high premiums for employees and their families, supported the Clinton proposals. Under the Health Security Act, the companies would save money because other businesses would share in the cost of health insurance.

The majority of health insurance companies—represented by HIAA—opposed the plan. But the biggest insurers, including CIGNA and Prudential, which had already established their own managed care operations, stood to gain from the millions of new subscribers the Clinton plan would bring to their networks. These companies withdrew from HIAA and launched their own lobbying effort to push for the plan.

Doctors, hospital administrators, and others in the health care industry objected to the managed care segments of the plan. The legislation promised to bring them millions of new customers who were now uninsured. With a national insurance plan in place, however, the market would put pressure on health care providers to join managed care groups, which would oversee their work and pay them set fees.

The members of at least five committees and subcommittees reviewed the Clinton bill and other health care proposals and worked to craft a compromise bill the full House and Senate would accept. Conservatives in the Republican Party, however, had no intention of cooperating on a health care bill. Determined to take control of Congress, they warned fellow Republicans to vote against any health care plan promoted by Democrats. If Democrats succeeded in passing the Health Security Act, they would use the accomplishment to strengthen their majority in Congress, the conservatives said. William Kristol, a leading conservative strategist, delivered his advice with a no-nonsense directness: kill the bill.

GROWING SUSPICION

President Clinton used his State of the Union address in January 1994 to try to revive public support for his health plan. Senator Bob Dole's televised response to the president's speech portrayed the Clinton proposals as "a massive overdose of Government control" for a health care crisis he said did not exist.

The Clinton Administration's inability to pinpoint the program's exact cost also undercut support for the plan. At various times, Americans were told that 30 percent or 40 percent of them would face higher insurance premiums under the plan. Most, however, would receive better coverage, and as budget director Leon Panetta noted, "100 percent of Americans can be expected to pay higher insurance premiums" without a federal plan in place.

Newspaper and magazine articles further weakened support for the Clinton plan. They characterized the plan as "dangerous" legislation that would cause "much unnecessary premature death and other suffering." The result was a growing suspicion of the Clinton proposals among Americans.

In February the Health Security Act lost more ground when the Business Roundtable, a highly regarded business group, and the U.S. Chamber of Commerce withdrew their support for the legislation. The National Association of Manufacturers followed suit, passing a resolution opposing the plan.

By April 1994 it was clear the Clinton plan was in trouble. Some Democrats abandoned the president's proposal for mandated premiums paid by employers to finance the plan. The plan's advocates suffered another blow when the powerful chair of the House Ways and Means Committee, Dan Rostenkowski, was forced to step down from his post after a federal grand jury indicted him on May 31, 1994, on charges of misuse of federal funds. He later served fifteen months in federal prison after pleading guilty to mail fraud.

On June 9 the Senate Labor and Human Resources Committee, chaired by longtime health reform advocate Senator Ted Kennedy, became the first to approve a health plan, releasing it for debate by the full House. Members voted 11 to 6 to support a plan with more benefits than Clinton's, but with voluntary rather than mandatory participation in health alliances.

With the health care bill still held up in other committees, the Clinton forces agreed to new compromises designed to win support from reluctant Democrats and moderate Republicans. But on June 28 Representative John Dingell announced that the Committee on Energy and Commerce could not come up with a health reform bill. Even with compromises negotiated by Dingell, the congressman could not win over Republican members, who opposed the employer mandate. A motion to support the bill failed by one vote.

Time was running out. As the 1994 midterm elections neared, polls indicated growing support for Republican candidates. Conservatives in the party grabbed the opportunity to pressure moderate Republicans in Congress to oppose the Clinton plan as a way to win support from voters in November. Meanwhile, groups that Clinton had counted on for support—retirees, labor, consumer organizations, and advocates in the health care field—focused on revising parts of the bill they disagreed with rather than supporting the overall concept, drawing sharp criticism from the First Lady.

HANGING BY A THREAD

Congress returned after the Fourth of July break, and on August 2 Senate Majority Leader Mitchell presented a plan that made big concessions to business by cutting mandated employer benefits. It aimed to provide coverage to 95 percent of Americans, not universal health insurance as the president had demanded. The Mitchell plan cost less than the Clinton proposal. The senator estimated his proposal would reduce government subsidies by $50 billion by the year 2000.

Mitchell's bill made it to the Senate floor. Debate on the legislation began on August 9. After two weeks of stalling and partisan bickering, Mitchell called for a break in the debate. Meanwhile, House leaders scheduled debate on a modified health bill based on a plan proposed by California Demo-

Senate Majority Leader George Mitchell (*left*) confers with Minority Leader Bob Dole during a committee session on the health care bill in 1994. Mitchell, who rejected Clinton's offer to nominate him for a seat on the U.S. Supreme Court to lead the health plan effort, later said the bill was dead.

crat Pete Stark. Consideration of a $30.2 billion crime bill interrupted their efforts. By the time the crime bill passed on August 25, House Democrats had backed away from the health bill, which they believed the Senate would reject.

By August 24, the *New York Times* reported that health reform legislation was "hanging by a fraying thread." Many believed it would take a miracle to pass any kind of health reform legislation before the end of the session.

On September 26, 1994—almost exactly a year after Clinton introduced his initiative to Congress—Senator Mitchell declared that health care reform was dead. Mitchell made the decision to end the effort after Republican leaders pledged to block NAFTA, which had already gone into effect, if the administration continued to push for health reform.

No health reform bill—not the Health Security Act or any

other version— made it to the floor of the House for debate during Clinton's presidency. "There were too many parts, too many new ideas, even for many policy experts to keep straight," Paul Starr, a Princeton professor and member of the Clinton health policy team, later wrote about the president's 1,342-page health initiative. The failure of the Clinton health insurance plan marked the defeat of all the other health care bills before Congress that session.

In November American voters replaced many Democrats with conservative Republicans and returned control of both houses of Congress to the Republicans for the first time in forty years. The Republican victory, coupled with Clinton's impeachment and subsequent trial after he lied about an affair with a White House intern, doomed any further effort for national health insurance during the Clinton presidency.

During Clinton's second term, Congress expanded health coverage for millions of the nation's children with the passage of the State Children's Health Insurance Program (SCHIP) in 1997. Sponsored by Senator Kennedy along with Senator Orrin Hatch, a Republican from Utah, the law provided federal funds to help states pay health insurance for low-income children. By 2000, more than 3.6 million children had been enrolled in the program. As part of the same legislation, Congress revised Medicare to allow retirees who chose to do so to enroll in managed care plans operated by private insurers and subsidized by the government.

But the demise of the Health Security Act spelled the end of the campaign for universal health insurance for fifteen years. "The collapse of health care reform in the first two years of the Clinton administration," said Starr, "will go down as one of the great lost political opportunities in American history."

CHAPTER SIX

Health Care: A Right of the People

In the first years of the new century, America's medical costs rose at least twice as fast as the rest of the economy. As health-related expenditures spiraled upward, the price of health insurance to help cover those costs also rose sharply.

The increases in premiums—a 131 percent hike in the cost of family coverage from 1999 to 2009—drove Americans to seek cheaper policies with less coverage and higher deductibles or to drop health insurance altogether. The majority of Americans relied on their employers to provide health insurance. Sixty percent of U.S. firms provided some form of health insurance for their workers in 2009, while retired workers received health benefits from 29 percent of their former employers. Squeezed by rising prices and a faltering economy, businesses began reducing benefits, turning to HMOs and other managed care plans, and requiring workers to share in the cost of premiums. Some smaller firms

Theresa Higginbotham and her four-year-old son, Jacob, pictured outside their home in Coal City, Indiana, in 2006, is one of the millions of Americans with no health coverage for their families. Higginbotham earns too much to qualify for state-paid health insurance but cannot afford insurance on her own.

discontinued all health care coverage for their employees, and fewer new companies offered health insurance benefits. Other companies hired part-time workers and independent consultants to avoid the health insurance costs required for a full-time staff. With union membership at an all-time low of 7.2 percent of the private workforce in 2009, labor negotiators no longer had the muscle to demand comprehensive health insurance for workers.

By 2007, 45.7 million Americans (15.3 percent of the total population of 298.7 million) were without health insurance coverage sometime during the year. Of those, about 9.7 million were not U.S. citizens (the census does not differentiate between legal and undocumented immigrants). For some of the uninsured, the loss of benefits lasted only for a short time. They went without insurance after losing their job but regained it when they got a new position that included health benefits. Others temporarily stopped paying premiums during financial hard times. But for many others—28 million who had no health insurance for at least two years—the lack of coverage was an ongoing problem.

SHARING PERSONAL EXPERIENCES

Members of Congress heard from desperate constituents with medical horror stories: parents sold their homes to pay for life-saving treatment for ill children. People faced bankruptcy as medical bills mounted. Hospitals struggled to cope with the soaring cost of treating uninsured patients. Employers and self-employed people paid increasingly higher insurance premiums, while workers settled for lower wages and dead-end jobs in exchange for health benefits.

Poverty, age, and race played a significant role in who had health insurance and access to medical care. About two-thirds of Americans without health insurance, thirty million people in 2002, earned low incomes, according to a report by the Agency of Healthcare Research and Quality, a federal research group. Many of these people worked on farms, in the food and service industries, or in construction—industries that did not usually provide health benefits. White and Asian Americans were more likely to have private insurance than black and Hispanic Americans. Hispanics, more of whom worked in industries without health benefits, were almost three times as likely as whites not to have health insurance.

People without insurance were much more likely to go without health care or seek medical help only for emergencies. The Urban Institute, a think tank focused on social trends and policy, estimated 22,000 Americans died in 2006 because they had no health insurance.

Even with coverage from Medicaid, the poorest Americans often had little access to vital health care services. While the federal government set rates for Medicare, which provided health care benefits for the elderly, the states were responsible for establishing rates for Medicaid, the health care program for low-income Americans. Medicaid paid so little to doctors and other health providers in some states that few health care providers were willing to accept Medicaid patients. In 2004, for example, Medicare paid New York doctors two to four times the amount they received for office visits for Medicaid patients.

As a result, many poor Americans—either on Medicaid or without coverage altogether—did not have a regular doctor to monitor their care. Poor communities had far fewer health care providers to service their needs than did wealthier areas. Although people without a regular doctor could go to hospitals for emergencies, those with chronic diseases such as asthma and diabetes, which required ongoing treatment, received inadequate care. In 2005 a woman living in the Bronx, New York City's poorest borough, was twenty times more likely to die from the effects of diabetes than a woman living in nearby Manhattan, one of the nation's wealthiest urban areas, according to a survey conducted by the city's Department of Health and Mental Hygiene.

Sixty-three percent of Americans without health coverage

were under the age of thirty-five in 2004. Despite the passage of the State Children's Health Insurance Program (SCHIP) in 1997, one in five American children went uninsured. President George W. Bush, a Republican who served from 2001 to 2009, twice vetoed amendments to expand SCHIP. Under President Obama's administration, Congress finally passed a bill in 2009 to increase funding and cover more children under the insurance plan.

President Bush put more focus on private industry, rather than government, to address rising costs in health care and the lack of access to medical care that came with them. In 2003 Congress passed the Medicare Prescription Drug Reform Act, based on a Bush-administration proposal to add drug coverage for retirees and people with disabilities. The act allowed Medicare recipients to buy an additional policy, with federal subsidies for poorer subscribers, from private insurers to cover prescription drugs.

RIGHT VS. RESPONSIBILITY

The two major Democratic candidates in the 2008 presidential race made national health insurance the centerpiece of their campaigns. Plans introduced by Hillary Clinton and Barack Obama both relied on a mix of employers, government, and individuals to pay for insurance for all. Both plans aimed to reduce premium costs by increasing the number of people with insurance. Both allowed Americans to choose between private insurance and a government-run plan (the so-called "public option").

John McCain, who became the Republican nominee, proposed a plan that would shift the responsibility of providing health insurance from employers to employees. It would also set up a national marketplace where Americans could shop for the best deals on health insurance with tax credits to help people pay for premiums.

Obama won the Democratic nomination, and he and McCain sparred over health care during the presidential debates. In October, during the second debate, McCain said, "I think [health care] is a responsibility, in this respect, in that we should have available and affordable health care to every American citizen, to every family member."

Obama framed the issue of national health care differently. "I think [health care] should be a right for every American," he said. He called on the personal experience of his mother to illustrate his point. "In a country as wealthy as ours, for us to have people who are going bankrupt because they can't pay their medical bills—for my mother to die of cancer at the age of fifty-three and have to spend the last months of her life in the hospital room arguing with insurance companies because they're saying that this may be a pre-existing condition and they don't have to pay her treatment, there's something fundamentally wrong about that."

In November voters gave Obama the chance to present his health care plan. The Illinois Democrat won the presidency with 53 percent of the popular vote. The new president faced a health care crisis of epic proportions. U.S. medical bills were the highest in the world. Federal analysts projected the United States would spend $2.5 trillion on health care in 2009, amounting to 17.6 percent of the nation's total economy and an average of $8,160 per person. Medicare and other government programs accounted for almost half of the health care spending.

The high prices, however, did not guarantee coverage for all. Millions of Americans remained without health insurance, had coverage for only part of the year, or had policies that did not cover many of their health needs. Other industrialized nations provided health coverage for all their citizens, but their medical care costs were well below that of the United States. America's high prices did not guarantee top-quality medical care either. According to a 2006 report by the World Health Organization (WHO), people in thirty-five other countries could expect to live longer than Americans, gave birth to babies who were more likely to survive, and received better treatment for chronic diseases such as asthma and diabetes as a result of better access to medical care.

President Obama gave only a passing reference to the cost and quality of American health care in his inaugural speech. Faced with a recession and trillion-dollar deficits, he first tackled the economic crisis with a stimulus package to bolster failing financial institutions.

The president opened his campaign for health care reform at a White House conference on March 4, 2009. More than 150 people attended, including congressional leaders of both parties, executives from insurance companies and other businesses, doctors and other health providers, labor representatives, and members of consumer groups.

At the outset, the new president focused on selling the idea of national health insurance rather than on a specific plan. "I just want to figure out what works," he said. He told the packed room that he was willing to accept compromises on the plan he detailed during the presidential campaign if it meant Congress would pass a health care reform bill. "If there is a way of getting this done where we're driving down costs and people are getting health insurance at an affordable rate and have choice of doctor, have flexibility in terms of their plans, and we could do that entirely through the market, I'd be happy to do it that way," Obama said. "If there was a way of doing it that involved more government regulation and involvement, I'm happy to do it that way as well."

Both versions—a plan that relied solely on private insurers and one with a government-run, public-option alternative—had their supporters and detractors. Several advocacy groups and some Democrats insisted a public option was the best way to ensure that prices stayed competitive and that everyone would have coverage. Other groups and most Republicans denounced any system that included more government programs. They argued that private insurers would go out of business if they had to compete with a government-run plan.

Several people, including the head of the American Hospital Association (AHA), argued that every American needed to participate in the insurance plan in order to spread the risk and decrease costs. Scott P. Serota, president of Blue Cross and Blue Shield Association, warned that national insurance would not work if healthy Americans could opt out and sign up only after they became ill. The nation should consider health insurance as "a responsibility on every individual, every institution and every enterprise in our society," declared AHA head Richard J. Umbdenstock.

A "SERIOUS EFFORT"

Senator Edward M. Kennedy, who attended the conference despite struggling with brain cancer, noted that he had witnessed many health reform initiatives over the years but never "the kind of serious effort" Obama had undertaken. "This time we will not fail," Kennedy predicted. The conference ended with Obama's pledge to cut the cost of health care and expand insurance coverage.

The president chose Kathleen Sebelius, Democratic governor of Kansas, to serve as secretary of health and human services, a key post in the health insurance campaign. The Senate approved her nomination in April.

While promoting health care reform, Obama left the drafting of the health bill to Congress. In the weeks following the White House conference, Democrats in Congress worked on several versions of a national health insurance plan. In less than a month, five committees had agreed to the major provisions included in the health reform bill:

- All Americans required to carry health insurance;
- Employers required to help pay for workers' insurance;
- Creation of a government plan offered as an alternative to private plans (the "public option").

Congress had not yet made the hardest decisions—how to pay for policies for the uninsured and how to coordinate the federal program with state laws on health insurance. The administration backed a public option, but it remained open to changes as members of the Obama team lobbied to win support. "The only nonnegotiable principle here is success. Everything else is negotiable," declared Rahm Emanuel, White House chief of staff.

Vice President Joseph Biden took on the role of White House ambassador to the Senate during the health-care campaign. A senator from Delaware for thirty-six years, Biden listened to what his former colleagues had to say about the issue and what they would and would not support. Senator Kennedy, chair of the Senate's Health, Education, Labor, and Pensions Committee, pushed his fellow legislators to vote on the health reform bill by the end of July. Democrat Max Baucus of Montana, chair of the Senate Finance Committee, also played a key role in the Senate campaign for health reform.

In the House, the Democratic chairmen of three key committees would steer the bill through Congress: Representatives George Miller of California, chair of the Education and Labor Committee; Henry A. Waxman, also of California, head of the Energy and Commerce Committee; and New York's Charles B. Rangel, chair of the powerful Committee on Ways and Means. House Speaker Nancy Pelosi of California and Senate Majority Leader Harry Reid of Nevada would lead the effort during the final push to get the bill passed.

The opponents and supporters, the political climate, and the dialogue had all shifted in the fifteen years between President Clinton's debacle and President Obama's strategic sessions. The American Medical Association, a heavy hitter in the fight against national health insurance, could no longer claim it spoke for 70 percent of the nation's doctors as it had in the 1960s when Congress enacted Medicare, or even 40 percent when the Clinton plan was introduced in the mid–1990s. Still a major player in the health field, the AMA represented 228,000 of the nation's doctors and medical students in 2009 (around 22 percent).

The economic burden on businesses, pressed by the rising cost of insuring their workers, had led many to support reform. The AHA lobbied for a health plan that would ease the burden on hospitals faced with shouldering the cost of treating uninsured patients. Even private insurance companies seemed to be willing to participate in the effort to reform the health care system.

During negotiations with Democratic leaders after the election, the insurance industry made two major concessions: to allow all Americans to buy health insurance and not to charge sick people higher premiums. In the past, private insurers limited their risk by rejecting people with costly medical conditions or charged them extra for insurance policies. Insurance lobbyists joined others involved in health care to hammer out differences on the issue at meetings organized by Kennedy aides and held twice a week in the Senate.

As Congress worked to fashion a bill—or several bills—to address the health care crisis, the AMA presented its terms. On June 10, 2009, the AMA informed the Senate Finance Committee that the doctors' group would oppose a public option and push for a plan that relied only on private insurers. AMA officials argued that a public option could force insurance companies out of business, interfere with patients' ability to choose their own doctors, and drive up costs.

During a speech at the AMA's annual conference in Chicago the following week, President Obama called the nation's rising health care costs "a ticking time bomb for the federal budget." If Congress did not act on the issue, he said, "premiums will climb higher, benefits will erode further, the rolls of the uninsured will swell to include millions more Americans, all of which will affect your practice." He defended his plan, telling the group, "If you like your doctor, you will be able to keep your doctor, period. If you like your health care plan, you'll be able to keep your health care plan, period. No one will take it away, no matter what." AMA members applauded the president but took a wait-and-see stance on his proposals.

On June 14 Democratic leaders in the House presented their health care bill, a joint product of all three committees reviewing the issue. Among its provisions, the measure required all Americans to have health insurance, purchased either from private insurers or from a government-run plan.

Government subsidies would assist those who could not afford premiums. Employers would have to offer health benefits or pay a penalty. Workers could opt for insurance under the federal program if their share of their employer's plan was too costly. The program would be paid for by cost-saving measures in Medicare (including a reduction in reimbursements to doctors), Medicaid, and similar government programs; changes in federal tax laws; and a tax levied on the wealthiest Americans.

The Congressional Budget Office reported that the bill would provide coverage to 37 million uninsured Americans at a cost of around $1 trillion over ten years. But it would also leave 17 million people—about half of whom were undocumented immigrants—still uninsured in 2019. People who qualified for Medicaid but failed to enroll would account for the rest of the uninsured. A few groups like the Amish, whose religion forbids participation in government programs such as Social Security, might be exempt from the plan.

Predictably, the bill drew fierce criticism from Republicans. They targeted the proposed taxes on the wealthy as well as the employer penalty for businesses not offering health packages. Representative John A. Boehner, the minority leader from Ohio, called the proposal "criminal malpractice" and charged that it would hurt small businesses that could not afford the additional benefits. Democrats countered that small businesses would benefit from the lower cost of health insurance.

Opposition to the bill also came from conservative Democrats in the House of Representatives known as the Blue Dog Coalition. Formed in 1994, the group of more than fifty members—mostly from the South—created an ominous crack in the Democratic majority's power in Congress.

By the end of July both Miller's Education and Labor Committee and Rangel's Ways and Means Committee had approved the bill and released it to the full House. Blue Dogs held seven seats on Waxman's Energy and Commerce Committee, however, and threatened to withhold their vote on the health bill. They voiced concerns about the high cost of the program, its effect on small businesses, and reduced Medicare reimbursements to doctors and hospitals, especially in rural areas. Without the support of the Blue Dogs, Waxman lacked the votes to get the bill past the committee and onto the House floor for debate. The standoff threatened to stall House action on the legislation until after the August summer break. The delay infuriated the plan's supporters. "Which is more important, money or live human beings with flesh and blood running through their veins, who cannot get health care?" asked Georgia Democrat Hank Johnson.

To get the bill back on track, the measure's supporters agreed to several concessions: an increase in some Medicare reimbursements, restrictions on coverage for abortions, and additional exemptions for businesses. On July 30 the Energy and Commerce Committee passed the compromise legislation, with the public option intact, on a vote of 35 to 24.

Meanwhile, the two Senate committees working on health reform considered two separate bills, one with a public option and one that relied only on private insurers. Kennedy's Health Committee, steered by Democrat Thomas Dodd of Connecticut in the absence of the ailing senator, passed the public-option measure on July 15, with all ten Republicans voting against the bill. Senator Baucus, who believed Republicans would never support a public option, worked with his finance committee to produce an alternate bill. The Baucus bill, developed by a team of three Democrats and three Republicans, would not be released by the committee until fall.

ANGRY PROTESTS

During Congress's recess in August, angry protesters disrupted town meetings set up to explain the Democrats' health plan. Opponents accused Obama of pushing for a health plan that rationed care to save money and created "death panels" to decide who could and could not get life-saving medical treatment. Sarah Palin, the Republican vice presidential candidate in 2008 and a favorite of the Tea Party movement—a conservative, anti-big-government group—frequently used the "death panel" label during her campaign against the health reform bill. "The America I know and love is not one in which my parents or my baby with Down's syndrome will have to stand in front of Obama's 'death panel' so his bureaucrats can decide . . . whether they are worthy of healthcare," Palin said in a statement posted on her Facebook page. "Such a system is downright evil."

No such provisions existed in the bill, but despite repeated assurances by the president and others that the Democratic plan would not "pull the plug on Grandma," the controversy raged on radio talk shows, Internet blogs, and at public demonstrations. Designed to fix a complex problem, the health care proposals were even bulkier than the Clinton legislation had been—the Senate plan grew to 2,074 pages. It was not easy to condense the document into simple terms.

In response to the public outcry, Obama went on the road to win support for national health insurance. "This is a quest for public opinion, just like an election," one policy expert observed. Appearing at town halls in New Hampshire, Montana, New York, and elsewhere, the president urged people

John Simmons (*left*) and David Williams express opposite views on health care reform during a rally in August 2009 in Atlanta. Several thousand people gathered in downtown Atlanta to state their opinions on the health care reform bill proposed by President Barack Obama and Congressional Democrats.

to ignore those using "scare tactics" to "mislead the American people."

The controversy took its toll on the president and his health initiative. Polls conducted in August showed that 52 percent of Americans disapproved of his handling of the health care issue. Even so, Americans continued to support changes in the health care system proposed under the Democratic plan.

Sixty percent or more of those responding said they wanted a public option, supported higher taxes on wealthy Americans to help pay for health care reform, and favored federal subsidies for health insurance. A majority (54 percent) thought businesses should be required to provide insurance or pay a penalty, but 68 percent said the government should not require individual Americans to have health insurance.

RENEWED COMMITMENT

On August 25, 2009, Senator Kennedy died. His death helped reinvigorate advocates of health care reform. At Kennedy's memorial service on August 28 Senator John Kerry, in an eloquent tribute to his friend, said, "For nearly four decades and all through his final days he labored with all of his might to make health care a right for all Americans, and we will do that in his honor."

Obama showed his own commitment to health care reform in an address to Congress and the nation on September 9. He pledged that everyone would have basic health insurance and likened the requirement to carry health insurance to laws in most states that require drivers to have auto insurance. "Improving our health care system only works if everybody does their part," the president said.

Obama estimated his plan would cost $900 billion over ten years (down from the original $1 trillion price tag). He signaled a willingness to abandon the public-option part of the plan if necessary and substitute it with other ways to keep premiums at affordable levels.

Later in the month Obama made marathon appearances on five different television talk shows, including popular late-night television, to explain the details of his insurance plan. The president's aggressive public relations campaign for health reform helped revive flagging spirits among supporters in Congress and elsewhere. According to polls released after the September 9 address, 67 percent of TV viewers said they supported the health reform provisions Obama outlined in his speech.

However, a later poll showed that Obama's marathon TV campaign had "done little to allay concerns" about the president's health care plan. Forty-six percent of those polled said they did not know enough about the plan to take a stand on it. Another 23 percent opposed it, while 30 percent supported it. Obama continued to win support for the job he was doing as president from a slim majority of Americans, 56 percent in the poll. A similar majority (52 percent) said they believed Barack Obama had better ideas on how to reform America's health care system than did Republicans in Congress. Only 27 percent thought Republicans had presented good ideas on solving the problem.

"THEIR FINEST MOMENT"

With Congress back in session, the Senate resumed work on the health proposal crafted by Senator Baucus. The plan, unveiled on September 16, contained most of the provisions outlined by Obama in his address, except a public-option program. It would cost an estimated $774 billion over ten years, but the Congressional Budget Office reported that the plan would help trim the federal deficit because of its cost-savings measures. The most conservative of the Democratic plans proposed in Congress, the Baucus bill cleared the Senate Finance Committee on October 13 by a 14 to 9 vote. Although Republican members of the committee helped fashion the bill, only one—Senator Olympia Snowe of Maine—voted to send the measure to the full Senate. Snowe later withdrew her support when Democrats added a public option to the bill.

In the House, Speaker Pelosi worked to shape a health reform bill that Blue Dogs and moderate Republicans would support. When it finally came before the House for a vote on November 7, 2009, the revised plan put limits on the public-option plan and restricted abortion coverage. House members debated the bill during a rare Saturday session at which emotions ran high. Several speakers brought their children and grandchildren with them to the podium. Supporters shared personal health care horror stories, while opponents attacked the bill with sharp rhetoric.

House Majority Leader Steny Hoyer began the debate with the story of one woman's trauma as she stood in a hospital and looked at cancer drugs that could save her life but that she could not afford because her insurance company denied her claim. Another constituent, a twelve-year-old boy, died after his tooth became infected and his family did not have the money to get it treated, Hoyer said. Opponents called the bill "a bad deal for average Americans" and "a gateway to a single-payer, government-controlled system" that "rations care" and "is anti-life."

In a last-minute revision to the bill, Representative Bart Stupak, a Democrat from Michigan, pushed through an amendment to prohibit health plans financed by the federal government from covering abortion. The amendment passed 240 to 194, after some pro-choice Democrats agreed to the concession to win approval for the overall bill. It was nearly midnight when members cast their votes on the health reform legislation itself. By only a five-vote margin, the House approved the reform bill 220 to 215. One Republican—Representative Joseph Cao of Louisiana—cast his vote for the measure. Thirty-nine Democrats, a majority from the South, joined Republicans in opposing the bill. President Obama told House supporters that they would consider the vote as "their finest moment in politics."

PASSING A SENATE PLAN

Major hurdles remained, however. Through several arduous weeks, Majority Leader Reid melded the two Senate bills into one. The resulting legislation had many of the same features as the House bill, including a public option. That provision was strengthened by the Congressional Budget Office's report that a health package with a public option would cost less than a proposal without one. "We are going to have a public option before this bill goes to the president's desk," Reid stated. "I believe the public option is so vitally important to create a level playing field and prevent the insurance companies from taking advantage of us."

The majority leader introduced the bill in the Senate on November 21. In an effort to pass the legislation before the Christmas recess, the Senate debated the bill for twenty-five days straight, taking only brief breaks on weekends. At times the senators extended their debate into the early morning hours after an all-day session.

The Democrats needed sixty votes to avoid a filibuster on the issue. Under the rules, senators can block a vote on legislation by debating around-the-clock. It takes sixty votes to stop such a filibuster. Republicans threatened to use the technique to derail the health reform bill. When Reid's bill came before the Senate in November, the Democrats had fifty-eight members, including Paul G. Kirk, who temporarily filled the late Senator Kennedy's seat until a special election could be held. Democrats also counted on two independent members, Joseph Lieberman of Connecticut and Bernard Sanders of Vermont, to vote with them.

The fact that every vote was crucial gave Lieberman and reluctant Democrats the power to demand concessions. Even before Reid brought the bill to the Senate floor, Lieberman threatened to join Republicans in a filibuster if the Democrats did not remove the public option and a proposal that allowed people to join Medicare at age fifty-five. Three Democrats—Senators Mary Landrieu of Louisiana, Blanche Lincoln of Arkansas, and Ben Nelson of Nebraska—pushed for their own concessions. All three joined Lieberman in his demand to remove a public-option provision.

Reid eventually threw in sweeteners for the dissenters in order to get a vote on the bill before Christmas. Landrieu, invoking her state's devastation from Hurricane Katrina, won a promise of at least $100 million in extra funds for Louisiana's Medicaid program. Nelson asked for and got a pledge that insurance companies could keep exemptions from anti-trust laws that regulated other industries. He also won more Medicaid money for his state and provisions that tightened restrictions on coverage for abortions.

On December 21 the revised bill overcame a major hurdle when the proposal's advocates won votes from sixty senators—the magic number to prevent a filibuster—to end debate and move toward final action. Three days later, after last-minute changes to appease liberal supporters, Reid's bill passed the Senate on a 60 to 39 vote. At sunrise on Christmas Eve, after an all-night session, all fifty-eight Democrats and two Independents voted for the bill. All forty Republicans opposed it, although Senator Jim Bunning of Kentucky missed roll call to cast his vote. Tears flowed when Senator Robert Byrd, the ninety-two-year-old Democrat from West

Virginia, cast a loud "Aye," and said, "This is for my friend, Ted Kennedy." An elated President Obama noted, "We are now incredibly close to making health insurance reform a reality in this country."

BROKERING AN HISTORIC BILL

Although the president's health reform initiative had overcome remarkable barriers, it still had one more big obstacle to surmount. Before legislation can become law, the Senate and the House must approve bills with identical provisions. Usually the two chambers hammer out a compromise bill in conference if they can, and the revised bill goes before the House and the Senate for a final vote. The House version of the health care bill contained a public option and other provisions that Democrats in the Senate, with no extra votes to spare, would be unlikely to accept. Democrats in the House, on the other hand, objected to the giveaways to Nebraska and stood firmly behind the public-option plan. Instead of going to conference with Republicans, who had pledged to do anything they could to block the legislation, Democrats decided to work out their own bill—acceptable to both House and Senate Democrats—to speed up the process.

Before that could be done, however, health reform advocates saw their dream of national health care jeopardized by a single vote. On January 19, 2010, Massachusetts voters elected Republican Scott Brown to fill Edward Kennedy's seat in the Senate, depriving the Democrats of the sixty votes they needed to prevent a filibuster. The death of the Senate's most passionate health care advocate ironically threatened the very cause he championed throughout his forty-seven years as a senator. If Democrats submitted a revised bill to the Senate, Republicans could filibuster and bury the legislation.

While some urged lawmakers to start over on health reform and others predicted the death of the initiative, House Speaker Pelosi and Senate Majority Leader Reid met with President Obama to resurrect the legislation. Their new strategy was to convince House Democrats to pass the Senate version of the bill. Democrats then would vote on a second bill that would include changes the House wanted made in the legislation. This "budget reconciliation bill" would then go to the Senate for approval. Since Senate rules prohibit filibusters on legislation of this type, the bill needed only a simple majority to pass.

A determined Speaker Pelosi set to work persuading skeptical Democrats to follow the strategy. At one point, House aides told reporters, Pelosi assigned herself the job of lobbying all sixty-eight Democrats the bill's backers had targeted as wavering on the measure. "We will go through the gate," Pelosi declared at a January 28 news conference. "If the gate is closed, we will go over the fence. If the fence is too high, we will pole vault in. If that doesn't work, we will parachute in. But we are going to get health care reform passed."

Opponents expressed equal determination to bury the bill. Republicans especially objected to the government's role in the Democrats' health insurance plan. They also opposed the bill's requirement that all Americans have health insurance. "If [Democrats] jam it through," said House Minority Leader Boehner, "I think they are going to face a firestorm from the American public."

The bill's supporters received a boost in February when Anthem Blue Cross announced it would raise rates in California by as much as 39 percent. Americans expressed outrage at the rate increase, and Democrats grabbed the opportunity to tout the need for health care reform. "The bottom line is that the status quo is good for the insurance industry and bad for America," President Obama said at a televised community meeting in Las Vegas on February 20. "And as bad as things are today, they'll only get worse if we fail to act. We'll see more and more Americans go without the coverage they need. We'll see exploding premiums and out-of-pocket costs burn through more and more family budgets."

On February 22, Obama outlined the revamped plan—called the Patient Protection and Affordable Care Act—that Democrats hoped to push through Congress. The act was the same as the Senate bill. Additional provisions and changes were included in the reconciliation bill. These included a ban on lifetime limits and denial of coverage because of medical conditions for all health plans within six months, higher initial subsidies for poor and moderate-income Americans, increases in fees imposed on insurance companies and other health-related firms to pay for the plan, and other changes. The revisions left in place extra funding for Louisiana but eliminated the Senate's special Nebraska deal. Instead, the act provided federal funds to help all states expand Medicaid benefits. Obama also increased the money allotted for community health centers to $11 billion. The final version also required insurers to spend 85 percent of the money collected from premiums on health care services or refund the money to policyholders.

The plan is estimated to cost $940 billion over ten years and is projected to reduce the deficit by $143 billion. One way the plan would accomplish that, its backers said, was by reducing employers' costs for health care. The savings would go toward better pay for workers. The increased income tax from the higher wages would help pay for the reforms.

During the days that followed, Obama put the spotlight on

the health care issue by telling Natoma Canfield's story at countless rallies across the country. The fifty-year-old self-employed Ohio woman wrote to the president after high premiums forced her to give up her health insurance. She feared she might lose her house if the cancer that afflicted her sixteen years before returned. In March she was rushed to a Cleveland hospital after she developed leukemia. Obama greeted Canfield's sister at an Ohio rally a week later and told the crowd, "I'm here because of Natoma."

As the vote on the revised bill loomed in the House, Obama and Democratic leaders counted votes and met with every member whose decision might be swayed. Representative Dennis J. Kucinich, an Ohio liberal who threatened to vote against the bill because it had no public-option plan, changed his mind after riding with the president aboard Air Force One to an Ohio rally. A day before the House vote, Obama made a last, fervent appeal to Democrats. "We're a day away," he said. "After a year of debate, after every argument has been made, by just about everybody, we're twenty-four hours away."

On March 21, the House convened to vote on the bill. Democratic leaders met at noon for a last-minute rally, where Representative John Lewis, a Georgia Democrat who had accompanied Martin Luther King Jr. on civil rights marches in the 1960s, cheered them on. The top Democrats linked arms and walked up the steps of the Capitol as angry protesters hurled insults at them and shouted "kill the bill." Inside they brokered yet another last-minute agreement, this one with Representative Stupak, who insisted on stronger limits on abortion coverage. Stupak supported the bill after President Obama agreed to issue an executive order that banned the use of federal money for insurance coverage of abortions.

The vote began around 10:30 p.m. When the crucial 216th

President Barack Obama signs the Health Care Reform Act on March 23, 2010, as supporters applaud.

vote needed for passage was cast, cheers of "Yes, we can!," Obama's campaign slogan, filled the room. In the final tally the House passed the bill 219 to 212. Shortly afterward, representatives passed the accompanying reconciliation bill by a vote of 220 to 211 and sent it to the Senate. After making minor changes in the measure, the Senate approved the reconciliation bill 56 to 43. Because there were no changes in the health reform bill itself, the Senate did not vote on that again. The House, in a final vote on the revisions to the reconciliation bill, voted its approval 220 to 207 on March 25. No Republicans voted for any of the measures.

President Obama signed the sweeping health care reform

bill into law on March 23. "Today, after almost a century of trying; today, after over a year of debate; today, after all the votes have been tallied—health insurance reform becomes law in the United States of America," Obama told an exuberant partisan crowd. "It is fitting that Congress passed this historic legislation this week. For as we mark the turning of spring, we also mark a new season in America."

ARMAGEDDON OR ACCESS TO DECENT CARE?

Since the passage of the Patient Protection and Affordable Care Act, Republicans in Congress and members of the Tea Party movement have threatened to repeal the legislation. On the same day President Obama signed the act, Florida and twelve other states filed a group lawsuit challenging the law in court, and Virginia sued on its own, charging that a federal requirement that states' citizens carry health insurance is unconstitutional. House Minority Leader Boehner compared the bill's passage to Armageddon. Some opponents predicted the bill would mark "the end of freedom." Others referred to the president as "Marxist in chief" and derisively nicknamed the new health reforms "Obamacare."

President Obama took the name-calling in stride, saying he had not witnessed Armageddon yet. "So after I signed the bill, I looked around," he told a crowd in Portland, Maine, a stop on yet another campaign to convince Americans that the health care law will benefit them. "I looked up in the sky to see if asteroids were coming. I looked at the ground to see if cracks had opened up in the earth. It turned out it was a pretty nice day. . . . Nobody had lost their doctor, nobody had pulled the plug on granny.

"This reform is not going to solve every problem with our health care system," the president noted. "It is a huge, complicated piece of business. . . . It's not going to bring down the cost of health care overnight. We're going to have to make some adjustments along the way. But it represents enormous progress. It enshrines the principle that every American should have the security of decent care, and that nobody should go bankrupt because they have a kid with a preexisting condition."

During mid-term elections in 2010, voters handed Republicans a majority in the House and gave them a total of forty-seven seats in the Senate. Republicans, who had made opposition to the health care act a key part of their platform, vowed to repeal or at least eliminate controversial provisions of the law. In particular, they targeted the act's requirement that all Americans carry health insurance and all employers carry coverage for their workers.

A poll conducted by Rasmussen in December 2010 revealed that 56 percent of likely voters favored repeal of the health care act, while 41 percent wanted to retain it. Among the reasons opponents of the act gave for supporting repeal was fear that the new health care law would increase the federal deficit, raise the cost of medical care, or decrease the quality of care. While a majority favored repeal, 52 percent of those polled said they preferred that Congress repeal only controversial parts of the law and keep the rest.

In January 2011 Republicans controlling the House of Representatives voted unanimously to repeal the health care reform act. Three Democrats, Dan Boren of Oklahoma, Mike Ross of Arkansas, and Mike McIntyre of North Carolina, joined the Republicans in voting for the measure, titled "The Repealing the Job-Killing Health Care Law Act."

Majority Leader Reid announced that the Senate would not consider any bill to repeal the health care reform act. The

Former Alaska governor Sarah Palin speaks at a gathering of Tea Party backers in Reno, Nevada, in October 2010. Members of the conservative movement were four times more likely than others to favor repeal of the health care reform act.

nonpartisan Congressional Budget Office reported that the health care reform act passed in 2010 would not "kill jobs." Instead, it would allow older workers to retire earlier by providing them more options for health insurance. President Obama pledged to "tweak" the health reform act to make it more acceptable to Americans. But he made it clear he would not sign any bill that repealed the entire act. Republicans pledged to cut off funds for the act and repeal sections of it.

Meanwhile, suits filed against the law continue to progress through the court system. In October 2010 a Michigan court dismissed a suit brought by the Thomas More Law Center that claimed the law unconstitutionally required employers and individuals to obtain health insurance. A federal judge dismissed a similar suit in December filed by Liberty University in Virginia, but another Virginia court struck down the requirement that citizens be required to buy health insurance. A fourth ruling in January 2011 against the law evened the score, with two judges for the health care reform act and two against. Judge Roger Vinson of the federal district court in Florida ruled on January 30, 2011, that the law's provision for mandatory health insurance violated the U.S. Constitution and that the entire law should be thrown out. By then at least twenty-five states had joined Florida in its suit to invalidate the law. The states claim that the Constitution's Commerce Clause cannot be used to force Americans to buy health insurance and that the act violates states' rights to regulate commerce within their borders. The Commerce Clause gives Congress the power to "regulate commerce with foreign nations, and among the several states, and with the Indian tribes." The two federal judges ruling in favor of the health care reform act were appointed by Democrats; Republicans appointed the two judges opposing the law.

Other suits challenged the law on a variety of grounds, including that it violated doctor-patient privileges, infringed on individual rights, and unconstitutionally increased taxes. At least one suit was expected to reach the Supreme Court.

Because many of the act's provisions will not go into effect for four years or more, citizens have not yet felt its full impact. The White House has set up a website (www.Health Care.gov) to explain the act and answer questions.

The Reverend Dr. Martin Luther King Jr. once said, "Of all the forms of inequality, injustice in health care is the most shocking and inhumane." Advocates of national health care are hoping that as Americans learn about the Patient Protection and Affordable Care Act and benefit from its provisions, they will resist opponents' efforts to dismantle it.

From Bill to Law

For a proposal to become a federal law, it must go through many steps:

In Congress:

1. A bill is proposed by a citizen, a legislator, the president, or another interested party. Most bills originate in the House and then are considered in the Senate.

2. A representative submits the bill to the House (the first reading). A senator submits it to the Senate. The person (or people) who introduces the bill is its main sponsor. Other lawmakers can become sponsors to show support for the bill. Each bill is read three times before the House or the Senate.

3. The bill is assigned a number and referred to the committee(s) and subcommittee(s) dealing with the topic. Each committee adopts its own rules, following guidelines of the House and the Senate. The committee chair controls scheduling for the bill.

4. The committees hold hearings if the bill is controversial or complex. Experts and members of the public may testify. Congress may compel witnesses to testify if they do not do so voluntarily.

5. The committee reviews the bill, discusses it, adds amendments, and makes other changes it deems necessary during markup sessions.

6. The committee votes on whether to support the bill, oppose it, or take no action on it and issues a report on its findings and recommendations.

7. A bill that receives a favorable committee report goes to the Rules Committee to be scheduled for consideration by the full House or Senate.

8. If the committee delays a bill or if the Rules Committee fails to schedule it, House members can sign a discharge motion and call for a vote on the matter. If a majority votes to release the bill from committee, it is scheduled on the calendar as any other bill would be. Senators may vote to discharge the bill from a committee as well. More commonly, though, a senator will add the bill as an amendment to an unrelated bill in order to get it past the committee blocking it. Or a senator can request that a bill be put directly on the Senate calendar, where it will be scheduled for debate. House and Senate members can also vote to suspend the rules and vote directly on a bill. Bills passed in this way must receive support from two thirds of those voting.

9. Members of both houses debate the bill. In the House, a chairperson moderates the discussion and each speaker's time is limited. Senators can speak on the issue for as long as they wish. Senators who want to block the bill may debate for hours in a tactic known as a filibuster. A three-fifths vote of the Senate is required to stop the filibuster (cloture), and talk on the bill is then limited to one hour per senator.

10. Following the debate, the bill is read section by section (the second reading). Members may propose amendments, which are voted on before the final bill comes up for a vote.

11. The full House and Senate then debate the entire bill and those amendments approved previously. Debate continues until a majority of members vote to "move the previous question" or approve a special resolution forcing a vote.

12. A full quorum—at least 218 members in the House, 51 in the Senate—must be present for a vote to be held. A member may request a formal count of members to ensure a quorum is on hand. Absent members are sought when there is no quorum.

13. Before final passage, opponents are given a last chance to propose amendments that alter the bill; the members vote on them.

14. A bill needs approval from a majority of those voting to pass. Members who do not want to take a stand on the issue may choose to abstain (not vote at all) or merely vote present.

15. If the House passes the bill, it goes on to the Senate. By that time, bills often have more than one hundred amendments attached to them. Occasionally, a Senate bill will go to the House.

16. If the bill passes in the same form in both the House and the Senate, it is sent to the clerk to be recorded.

17. If the Senate and the House version differ, the Senate sends the bill to the House with the request that members approve the changes.

18. If the two houses disagree on the changes, the bill may go to conference, where members appointed by the House and the Senate work out a compromise if possible.

19. The House and the Senate vote on the revised bill agreed to in conference. Further amendments may be added and the process repeated if the Senate and the House version of the bill differ.

20. The bill goes to the president for a signature.

To the President:

1. If the president signs the bill, it becomes law.

2. If the president vetoes the bill, it goes back to Congress, which can override his veto with a two-thirds vote in both houses.

3. If the president takes no action, the bill automatically becomes law after ten days if Congress is still in session.

4. If Congress adjourns and the president has taken no action on the bill within ten days, it does not become law. This is known as a pocket veto.

The time from introduction of the bill to the signing can range from several months to the entire two-year session. If a bill does not win approval during the session, it can be reintroduced in the next Congress, where it will have to go through the whole process again.

Notes

Chapter One

p. 15, "to care for . . . ," "The Story of the Creation of the Nation's First Hospital," Penn Medicine, www.uphs.upenn.edu/paharc/features/creation.html

p. 18, "the germ *theory* . . . ," Walter B. Goldfarb, "History of Surgery in Maine," *Archives of Surgery*, vol. 136, April 2001, 448–452.

p. 18, "The number of . . . ," Francis Lasseter, "A Nursing Legacy—Political Activities at the Turn of the Century," *AORN Journal*, November 1999.

pp. 21–22, "perhaps the people . . . ," Theodore Roosevelt, "Address by Theodore Roosevelt Before the Convention of the National Progressive Party," Chicago, August 1912, www.ssa.gov/history/trspeech.html

p. 24, "statistics on workers' . . . ," *New York Times*, "Health Insurance for New York's Workers," January 30, 1916, Sunday Magazine, 8.

p. 24, "No other social . . . ," "Industrial insurance," *Journal of the American Medical Association*, 1916, 66:433, cited in Judith Walzer Leavitt and Ronald L. Numbers, eds., *Sickness and Health in America: Readings in the History of Medicine and Public Health*, Madison: University of Wisconsin Press, 1997, 270.

p. 24, "study this important . . . ," *New York Times*, "Health Insurance for New York's Workers," January 30, 1916, Sunday Magazine, 8.

p. 24, "a servant of . . . ," *New York Times*, "Health Insurance for New York's Workers."

p. 25, "That the United States . . . ," *New York Times*, "Health Insurance for New York's Workers."

p. 25, "The bill will find . . . ," *New York Times*, "Health Insurance for New York's Workers."

p. 26, "well meaning but . . . ," *New York Times*, "Health Insurance for New York's Workers."

p. 26, "a menace to the rights . . . ," Thomas Daschle, *Critical: What We Can Do About the Health-Care Crisis*, New York: Thomas Dunne Books, 2008, 48.

p. 27, "At present . . . ," Jill Lepore, "Preexisting Condition," *The New Yorker*, December 7, 2009, www.newyorker.com/talk/comment/2009/12/07/091207 taco_talk_lepore

p. 27, "made in Germany . . . ," "A Symposium on Compulsory Health Insurance Presented Before the Medical Society of the County of Kings, Oct. 21, 1919," *Long Island Medical Journal*, 1919, 13: 445, cited in Leavitt and Numbers, *Sickness and Health in America*.

p. 27, "UnAmerican, Unsafe . . . ," Lepore, "Preexisting Condition."

pp. 27–28, "would spell social . . . ," Lepore, "Preexisting Condition."

p. 29, "pernicious and un-American." *New York Times*, "Republican Women in Tilt with Sweet," April 8, 1920, 11.

p. 30, "Bolshevist [communist] propaganda . . . ," *New York Times*, "Republican Women in Tilt with Sweet," April 8, 1920, 11.

p. 31, "a dead issue . . . ," Leavitt and Numbers, eds., *Sickness and Health in America*.

Chapter Two

p. 33, "By 1934 . . . ," Joseph S. Ross, "The Committee on the Costs of Medical Care and the History of Health Insurance in the United States," *Einstein Quarterly*, 19, 2002, 130.

pp. 34–35, "In this arrangement . . . ," Editorial, "American Medical Association Joins American Hospital Association in Approving Pre-payment Medical as well as Hospital Service," *Journal of the National Medical Association*, 30:4, November 1938, 160–161.

p. 35, "In this arrangement . . . ," Editorial, "American Medical Association Joins American Hospital Association in Approving Pre-payment Medical as well as Hospital Service."

p. 37, "an incitement . . . ," Karen S. Palmer, "A Brief History: Universal Health Care Efforts in the U.S.," Physicians for a National Health Program, Spring 1999, www.pnhp.org/facts/a_brief_history_universal_health_care_efforts_in_the_us.php?page=all

p. 37, "socialized medicine . . . ," Ross, "The Committee on the Costs of Medical Care and the History of Health Insurance in the United States."

p. 38, "When he begins . . . ," Jean Edward Smith, *FDR*, New York: Random House, 2007, 351.

p. 39, "A poll conducted . . . ," "Social Security History," Social Security Online History Pages, www.ssa.gov/history/corningchap3.html

p. 41, "the right to adequate . . . ," Harry S. Truman, "Special Message to the Congress Recommending a Comprehensive Health Program," November 19, 1945, www.trumanlibrary.org/publicpapers/index.php?pid=483

p. 42, "The rising cost . . . ," "President Harry S. Truman's Federal Health Insurance Plan," *California and Western Medicine*, 63:6, December 1945, 270–274.

pp. 42–43, "What I am recommending . . . ," Harry S. Truman, "Special Message to the Congress Recommending a Comprehensive Health Program."

p. 43, "Of those who knew . . . ," Monte M. Poen, *Harry S. Truman Versus the Medical Lobby: The Genesis of Medicare*, Columbia, MO: University of Missouri, 1979, 30, 167.

p. 44, "The doctors' organization . . . ," Palmer, "A Brief History: Universal Health Care Efforts in the U.S."

p. 45, "They accused everyone . . . ," Poen, "National Health Insurance," in Richard S. Kirkendall, (ed.), *The Harry S. Truman Encyclopedia*, Boston: G. K. Hall & Co., 1989, 251.

pp. 46–47, "Is it un-American . . . ," Harry S. Truman, "Address in Indianapolis at the Indiana World War Memorial," October 15, 1948, John T. Woolley and Gerhard Peters, *The American Presidency Project* [online], Santa Barbara, CA, www.presidency.ucsb.edu/ws/?pid=13052

p. 47, "69 percent of those . . . ," "Social Security History," Social Security Online History Pages.

pp. 47–48, "A *Fortune* magazine poll . . . ," Peter A. Corning, "The Evolution of Medicare . . . from idea to law," Social Security Administration, 1969, www.ssa. gov/history/corningchap3.html

p. 48, "But a Gallup poll . . . ," "Social Security History," Social Security Online History Pages.

p. 48, "The following year . . . ," Brian Hensel, "Harry Truman's Reluctance in Going Public for National Health Insurance," paper presented at the annual meeting of the International Communication Association, New Orleans Sheraton, New Orleans, LA, May 27, 2004, www.allacademic.com/meta/p113371_index.html

p. 48, "25 percent in 1946 . . . ," Greg Scandlen, "Defined Contribution Health Insurance," National Center for Policy Analysis, No. 154, October 26, 2000, www. ncpa.org/pub/bg154

p. 48, "I have had some bitter . . . ," "Social Security History," Social Security Online History Pages.

p. 49, "In 1950, 12 million . . . ," "Social Security History," Social Security Online History Pages.

p. 49, "I suppose I could . . . ," Norbert Goldfield, "National Health Reform Advocates Retrench and Prepare for Medicare," *Physician Executive*, May–June 1993, http://findarticles.com/p/articles/mi_m0843/is_n3_v19/ai_14235769/? tag=content;col1

p. 50, "Many of our . . . ," Dwight D. Eisenhower, "Recommendations to Improve the Health of the American People," January 18, 1954, John T. Woolley and Gerhard Peters, The American Presidency Project [online], Santa Barbara, CA, www.presidency.ucsb.edu/ws/?pid=10399.

p. 51, "no Government subsidy . . . ," Eisenhower, "Recommendations to Improve the Health of the American People."

p. 51, "socialist trend . . . ," Goldfield, "National Health Reform Advocates Retrench and Prepare for Medicare."

Chapter Three

p. 54, "We've got a President . . . ," "Welfare: Aid for the Aged," *Time* magazine, April 4, 1960, www.time.com/time/magazine/article/0,9171,869428,00.html

p. 55, "to adequate medical care . . . ," Democratic Party Platform of 1960, July 11, 1960, John T. Woolley and Gerhard Peters, *The American Presidency Project* [online], Santa Barbara, CA, www.presidency.ucsb.edu/ws/?pid=29602

p. 55, "burdensome costs . . . ," Republican Party Platform of 1960, July 25, 1960, John T. Woolley and Gerhard Peters, *The American Presidency Project* [online], Santa Barbara, CA, www.presidency.ucsb.edu/ws/index.php?pid=25839

pp. 58–59, "The need . . . ," Natalie Jaffe, "Hundreds Attend Hearing for Aged," *New York Times*, January 19, 1964, 63.

p. 56, Ronald Reagan, "Ronald Reagan Speaks Out Against Socialized Medicine," produced by the American Medical Association, 1961. YouTube, www.youtube. com/watch?v=z43NCL6Fxug

p. 56, Damon Adams, "Reagan Praised as Medicine's Friend," *American Medical*

News, American Medical Association, June 21, 2004, www.ama-assn.org/amed
news/2004/06/21/prsd0621.htm

p. 56, Robert W. Watson, *White House Studies Compendium*, vol. 5, New York:
Nova Science Publishers Inc., 2008, 31.

p. 61, "The results showed . . . ," Philip Benjamin, "Elderly United as Lobby Force,"
New York Times, May 21, 1962, 22.

p. 61, "the real daddy . . . ," Mark K. Updegrove, *Second Acts: Presidential Lives and
Legacies after the White House*, Guilford, CT: Lyons Press, 2006, 25.

Chapter Four

p. 65, "partnership program . . . ," Daniel Schorr, "National Health Insurance," *CBS
News*, February 18, 1971, Youtube, www.youtube.com/watch?v=iGKkPEvD2OM

p. 66, "My child was . . . ," Edward M. Kennedy, "Ted Kennedy on Health Care,"
speech, Montgomery County (Pennsylvania) Democratic Committee annual
spring reception, April 3, 2008, www.youtube.com/watch?v=PrJVbCzJH6c

p. 71, "These gaps . . . ," Richard Nixon, "President Richard Nixon's Special Message
to the Congress Proposing a Comprehensive Health Insurance Plan," February
6, 1974, John T. Woolley and Gerhard Peters, The American Presidency Project
[online], Santa Barbara, CA: University of California (hosted), Gerhard Peters
(database), www.presidency.ucsb.edu/ws/?pid=4337

pp. 71–72, "Comprehensive health insurance . . . ," Harold M. Schmeck Jr., "Nixon
Sees Passage in '74 of a Health Insurance Plan," *New York Times*, February 6,
1974, 16.

p. 72, "either late this year . . . ," Catherine Mackin, "National Health Insurance,"
NBC April 24, 1974, Youtube, www.youtube.com/watch?v=iGKkPEvD2OM

p. 74, "In retrospect . . . ," Sam Stein, "When Kennedy Nearly Achieved the 'Cause
of His Life': Health Care Reform with Nixon," *Huffington Post*, August 26, 2009,
www.huffingtonpost.com/2009/08/26/when-kennedy-nearly-achie_n_269935.
html

Chapter Five

p. 75, "quality health care . . . ," Republican Party Platform of 1976, August 18, 1976,
John T. Woolley and Gerhard Peters, *The American Presidency Project* [online],
Santa Barbara, CA, www.presidency.ucsb.edu/ws/index.php?pid=25843

p. 77, "In response . . . ," Philip J. Hilts, "Corporate Chiefs See Need for U.S. Health-
Care Action," *New York Times*, April 8, 1991, www.nytimes.com/1991/04/08/
business/corporate-chiefs-see-need-for-us-health-care-action.html

p. 78, "All of our efforts . . . ," Colin Gordon, *Dead on Arrival*, Princeton, NJ: Princeton
University Press, 2004, 163.

p. 78, "take on the health . . . ," Bill Clinton, "Address Accepting the Presidential
Nomination at the Democratic National Convention in New York," July 16, 1992,
John T. Woolley and Gerhard Peters, *The American Presidency Project* [online],
Santa Barbara, CA, www.presidency.ucsb.edu/ws/?pid=25958

p. 78, "Half of Americans . . . ," Erik Eckholm, "Health Benefits Found to Deter
Switches in Jobs," *New York Times*, September 26, 1991, 1.

p. 79, "One health care . . . ," Joseph Nocera, "The Tarnished Darlings of Wall

Street," *New York Times*, January 4, 1998, www.nytimes.com/1998/01/04/opinion/the-tarnished-darlings-of-wall-street.html?scp=4&sq=Wall+Street+Health+care&st=nyt

p. 79, "A *New York Times* . . . ," Milt Freudenheim, "IRS Studies Pay of Hospital Chiefs," *New York Times*, April 14, 1992, www.nytimes.com/1992/04/14/business/business-and-health-irs-studies-pay-of-hospital-chiefs.html?scp=6&sq=chief+executive+of+health+care+annual+salaries&st=nyt

p. 79, "*Forbes* magazine . . . ," "CEO Compensation," Forbes online, www.forbes.com

p. 79, "At the top . . . ," Matt Kapp, "The Sick Business of Health-Care Profiteering," *Vanity Fair*, September 24, 2009, www.vanityfair.com/politics/features/2009/09/health-care200909

p. 81, "great lies . . . ," Adam Clymer, "Hillary Clinton Accuses Insurers of Lying about Health Proposal," *New York Times*, November 2, 1993, 1.

p. 82, "If they choose . . . ," "Harry and Louise on Clinton's Health Plan," www.youtube.com/watch?v=Dt31nhleeCg

p. 82, "The Health Insurance Association . . . ," Natasha Singer, "Harry and Louise Return, With a New Message," *New York Times*, July 17, 2009, B3.

p. 82, "It looks like . . . ," "Harry and Louise on Clinton's Health Plan."

pp. 83–84, "At long last . . . ," Bill Clinton, "Address on Health Care Reform," September 22, 1993, Miller Center of Public Affairs, http://millercenter.org/scripps/archive/speeches/detail/3926

p. 84, "It's a great . . . ," Clifford Krauss, "Clinton's Health Plan: Reaction; Congress Praises President's Plan But Is Wary of Taxes and Costs," *New York Times*, September 23, 1993, www.nytimes.com/1993/09/23/us/clinton-s-health-plan-reaction-congress-praises-president-s-plan-but-wary-taxes.html

p. 84, "It is a bizarre . . . ," Adam Clymer, "Clinton's Health Plan; First Republican Support Health Plan," *New York Times*, September 30, 1993, www.nytimes.com/1993/09/30/us/clinton-s-health-plan-first-republican-supports-health-plan.html

p. 85, "do away—forever . . . ," Adam Clymer, "Senate Approves Brady Legislation and Trade Accord," *New York Times*, November 21, 1993, www.nytimes.com/1993/11/21/us/senate-approves-brady-legislation-and-trade-accord.html

p. 86, "a massive overdose . . . ," "Clinton Timeline," *MacNeil/Lehrer NewsHour*, PBS, 1996, www.pbs.org/newshour/forum/may96/background/health_debate_page1.html

p. 87, "100 percent . . . ," Adam Clymer, "Administration Offers New Math to Bolster Health Plan's Appeal," *New York Times*, November 5, 1993, 1.

p. 87, "They characterized . . . ," George Will, "The Clintons' Lethal Paternalism," *Newsweek*, February 7, 1994, www.newsweek.com/1994/02/06/the-clintons-lethal-paternalism.html

p. 89, "hanging by a fraying . . . ," Adam Clymer, "The Health Care Debate: The Negotiations," *New York Times*, August 24, 1994, 1.

p. 90, "There were too many . . . ," Paul Starr, "What Happened to Health Care Reform?" *The American Prospect*, no. 20, Winter 1995, 20–31.

p. 90, "the collapse . . . ," Starr, "What Happened to Health Care Reform?"

Chapter Six

p. 91, "a 131 percent . . . ," "Employer Health Benefits, 2009 Annual Survey," Kaiser Family Foundation and Health Research & Educational Trust, #7936, 4, www.kff.org

p. 91, "Sixty percent . . . ," "Employer Health Benefits, 2009 Annual Survey."

p. 93, "By 2007, 45.7 million . . . ," Carmen DeNavas-Wait, Bernadette D. Proctor, and Jessica C. Smith, "Income, Poverty, and Health Insurance Coverage in the United States: 2007," U.S. Census Bureau, August 2008, 19–27.

p. 93, "Poverty, age, and race . . . ," Michelle Roberts, "Racial and Ethnic Differences in Health Insurance Coverage and Usual Source of Health Care, 2002," Rockville, MD: Agency of Healthcare Research and Quality, 2006. MEPS Chartbook No. 14, AHRQ Pub. No. 06-0004, www.ahrq.gov

p. 94, "The Urban Institute . . . ," Stan Dorn, "Uninsured and Dying Because of It: Updating the Institute of Medicine Analysis on the Impact of Uninsurance on Mortality," The Urban Institute: Washington, DC, January 8, 2008, www.urban.org/publications/411588.html

p. 94, "In 2004 . . . ," Neil Calman, "Making Health Equality a Reality: The Bronx Takes Action," *Health Affairs*, 24: 2, 2005, 491–498.

p. 94, "In 2005 . . . ," New York City Department of Health and Mental Hygiene, *Health Disparities in New York City*, 2004, www.nyc.gov/html/doh/pdf/epi/disparities-2004.pdf (1 February 2005). Cited in Neil Calman, "Making Health Equality a Reality: The Bronx Takes Action."

pp. 94–95, "Sixty-three percent . . . ," "Overview of the Uninsured in the United States: An Analysis of the 2005 Current Population Survey," U.S. Department of Health and Human Services, September 22, 2005, http://aspe.hhs.gov/health/reports/05/uninsured-cps

p. 96, "I think [health care] is a responsibility . . . ," "2008 Presidential Candidate Health Care Proposals: Side-by-Side Summary," health08.0rg, Kaiser Family Foundation, www.health08.org/sidebyside_results.cfm?c=5&c=16

p. 96, "I think [health care] should . . . ," "2008 Presidential Candidate Health Care Proposals: Side-by-Side Summary."

p. 96, "Federal analysts . . . ," "National Health Expenditure Projections 2008–2018," Centers for Medicare and Medicaid Services, www.cms.gov/NationalHealthExpendData/downloads/proj2008.pdf

p. 97, "People in thirty-five . . . ," Ellen Nolte and C. Martin McKee, "Measuring the Health of Nations: Updating an Earlier Analysis," *Health Affairs*, January/February 2008; 27(1), 58–71.

pp. 97–98, "I just want to . . . ," Robert Pear and Sheryl Gay Stolbert, "Obama Says He Is Open to Altering Health Plan," *New York Times*, March 5, 2009, A14.

p. 98, "a responsibility on every . . . ," Pear and Stolbert, "Obama Says He Is Open to Altering Health Plan."

p. 98, "the kind of serious . . . ," Robert Pear and David Stout, "Obama Vows to End Stalemate on Health Care," *New York Times*, March 6, 2009, www.nytimes.com

p. 99, "The only nonnegotiable . . . ," Matt Bai, "Taking the Hill," *New York Times*, June 2, 2009, MM30.

p. 100, "Still a major . . . ," Andis Robeznieks, "AMA Profit Grows Despite Membership Decline," *Modern Physician*, June 7, 2010, https://home.modernhealthcare.com

p. 101, "During a speech . . . ," Robert Pear and David M. Herszenhorn, "A Primer on the Details of Health Care Reform," *New York Times*, August 10, 2009, A8.

p. 102, "criminal malpractice . . . ," Robert Pear and David M. Herszenhorn, "House Health Plan Outlines Higher Taxes on Rich," *New York Times*, July 15, 2009, A1.

p. 103, "Which is more important . . . ," Robert Pear and David M. Herszenhorn, "Democrats' Divide Fuels Turmoil on Health Care," *New York Times*, July 25, 2009, A13.

p. 104, "The America I know . . . ," Sarah Palin, "Statement on the Current Health Care Debate, Facebook page, cited in Jake Tapper, "Palin Paints Picture of 'Obama Death Panel' Giving Thumbs Down to Trig," *ABC News*, August 7, 2009, http://blogs.abcnews.com/politicalpunch/2009/08/palin-paints-picture-of-obama-death-panel-giving-thumbs-down-to-trig.html

pp. 104–105, "This is a quest . . . ," Katharine Q. Seelye, "For Obama, Selling Health Care Is Now an Inside-Outside Game," *New York Times*, October 10, 2009, http://prescriptions.blogs.nytimes.com/2009/10/10/for-obama-selling-health-care-is-now-an-inside-outside-game/?scp=1&sq=Obama%20addresses%20AMA&st=cse

p. 105, "the president urged . . . ," Laura Conway, "Obama Says His Health Plan Won't 'Pull the Plug on Grandma,'" National Public Radio, August 11, 2009.

pp. 105–106, "Polls conducted . . . ," "Scrap Health Care Reform If It Adds to Deficit, U.S. Voters Tell Quinnipiac University National Poll," Quinnipiac University, August 5, 2009, www.quinnipiac.edu/x1295.xml?ReleaseID=1357

p. 106, "For nearly four . . . ," "Edward Kennedy Memorial Service," August 28, 2009, YouTube, www.youtube.com/watch?v=zG4eAkdnBj4

p. 106, "Improving our health . . . ," Barack Obama, "Remarks by the President to a Joint Session of Congress on Health Care," September 9, 2009, White House, www.whitehouse.gov/the-press-office/remarks-president-a-joint-session-congress-health-care

p. 107, "According to polls . . . ," "Obama Wins with Speech-Watchers, Poll Says," CNN, September 10, 2009, www.cnn.com/2009/POLITICS/09/09/poll.obama.speech/index.html

p. 107, "a later poll . . . ," Adam Nagourney and Dalia Sussman, "New York Times/CBS Poll: Confusion Over Health Care," *New York Times*, September 24, 2009, 1.

p. 108, "Opponents called . . . ," *Congressional Record*, 111th Cong., 1st sess., House, November 7, 2009, H12835–12836.

p. 109, "their finest . . . ," Adamy and Bendavid, "House Passes Health-Care Reform Bill in Historic Vote," CNN, March 21, 2010, http://articles.cnn.com/2010-03-21/politics/health.care.main_1_health-care-entire-house-democratic-caucus-pre-existing-conditions?_s=PM:POLITICS

p. 109, "We are going . . . ," J. Taylor Rushing, "Reid, Baucus Ready to Split on Public Option for Healthcare as Vote Nears," *The Hill*, October 5, 2009, http://thehill.com/homenews/senate/61561-reid-baucus-ready-to-split-on-public-option

p. 111, "Aye . . . ," Kathy Kiely, "Senate Passes Health Care Bill," *USA Today*, December 25, 2009, www.usatoday.com/news/washington/2009-12-23-health-care_N.htm

p. 112, "We will go . . . ," Sheryl Gay Stolberg, Jeff Zeleny, and Carl Hulse, "Health

Vote Caps a Journey Back from the Brink," *New York Times*, March 21, 2010, A1.

p. 112, "If [Democrats] . . . ," Robert Pear and David M. Herszenhorn, "A New Search for Consensus on Health Care Bill," *New York Times*, January 21, 2010, 1.

pp. 112–113, "The bottom line . . . ," Jared Allen, "Obama Slams Anthem Rate Increase in Pushing Healthcare Bill," *The Hill*, February 20, 2010, http://thehill.com/homenews/administration/82417-obama-slams-anthem-rate-increase-in-pushing-healthcare-bill

p. 113, "The plan is estimated . . . ," Jill Jackson and John Nolen, "Health Care Reform Bill Summary: A Look at What's in the Bill," *CBS News*, March 23, 2010, www.cbsnews.com/8301-503544_162-20000846-503544.html

p. 114, "I'm here . . . ," Andrew Malcolm, *Los Angeles Times*, "The Good News Behind Obama's Sad Natoma Canfield Story," March 16, 2010, http://latimesblogs.latimes.com/washington/2010/03/obama-healthcare-natoma.html

p. 114, "We're a day . . . ," Stolberg et al., "Health Vote Caps a Journey Back from the Brink."

pp. 115–116, "Today, after almost . . . ," Peter Nicholas and Christi Parsons, "President Obama Signs Healthcare Overhaul into Law," *Los Angeles Times*, March 24, 2010, http://articles.latimes.com/2010/mar/24/nation/la-na-health-signing24-2010mar24

p. 116, "So after I . . . ," Keith Shortall, "Obama Addresses Enthusiastic Crowd at the Portland Expo," *Maine Things Considered*, April 1, 2010.

pp. 116–117, "This reform . . . ," Keith Shortall, "Obama Addresses Enthusiastic Crowd at the Portland Expo," *Maine Things Considered*, April 1, 2010.

p. 117, "A poll conducted . . . ," "Health Care Law," Rasmussen Reports, December 7, 2010, www.rasmussenreports.com/public_content/politics/current_events/healthcare/health_care_law

p. 119, "Of all the forms . . . ," Martin Luther King Jr. "Presentation at the Second National Convention of the Medical Committee for Human Rights," Chicago, March 25, 1966. Cited on National Center for Biotechnology Information website, www.ncbi.nlm.nih.gov/pmc/articles/PMC2464852/#ref1

All websites were accurate and accessible as of February 4, 2011.

Further Information

AUDIO/VIDEO

Kennedy, Edward M. "Ted Kennedy on Health Care," speech, April 3, 2008, YouTube, www.youtube.com/watch?v=PrJVbCzJH6c

The Legislative Branch (United States Government). Schlessinger Media, 2002 (video).

WGBH, "Sick Around the World," *Frontline*, PBS, April 15, 2008, www.pbs.org/wgbh/pages/frontline/sickaroundtheworld

BOOKS

Blashfield, Jean F. *Hillary Clinton*. New York: Marshall Cavendish, 2010.

Burgan, Michael. *Barack Obama*. Chicago: Heinemann-Raintree, 2009.

Epstein, Dwayne. *Nancy Pelosi*. San Diego: Lucent, 2009.

Hamilton, Lee H. *How Congress Works and Why You Should Care*. Bloomington: Indiana University Press, 2004.

Harris, Nancy. *Does the United States Need a National Health Insurance Policy?* Farmington Hills, MI: Greenhaven Press, 2005.

Hunnicutt, Susan. *Universal Health Care*. Farmington Hills, MI: Greenhaven Press, 2010.

Kowalski, Kathiann M. *National Health Care*. New York: Marshall Cavendish, 2008.

Naden, Corinne. *Health Care: A Right or a Privilege?*. New York: Marshall Cavendish, 2010.

Pach, Chester J. *The Johnson Years*. New York: Facts on File, 2005.

Sapet, Kerrily. *Ted Kennedy*. Greensboro, NC: Morgan Reynolds Publishing, 2009.

Uebelhor, Tracy S. *The Truman Years*. New York: Facts on File, 2005.

Worth, Richard. *Social Security Act*. New York: Marshall Cavendish, 2011.

WEBSITES
American Presidency Project
www.presidency.ucsb.edu

Centers for Medicare and Medicaid Services
www.cms.gov

DATA.gov
www.data.gov

Kaiser Family Foundation
kff.org

National Institutes of Health
www.nih.gov

Social Security Administration
www.ssa.gov

Thomas, Library of Congress legislative information
http://thomas.loc.gov

U.S. Government Site on Health Care Reform Act Provisions
www.HealthCare.gov

White House
www.whitehouse.gov

All websites were accurate and accessible as of February 4, 2011.

Bibliography

AUDIO/VIDEO

"Barack Obama on David Letterman," September 21, 2009, *The Late Show with David Letterman*, CBS.

"Edward Kennedy Memorial Service," August 28, 2009, www.youtube. com/watch?v=zG4eAkdnBj4

"Harry and Louise on Clinton's Health Plan." www.youtube.com/watch?v =Dt31 nhleeCg

Kennedy, Edward M. "Ted Kennedy on Health Care," speech, Montgomery County (Pennsylvania) Democratic Committee annual spring reception, April 3, 2008.

Mackin, Catherine. "National Health Insurance," *NBC*, April 24, 1974.

Reagan, Ronald. "Ronald Reagan Speaks Out Against Socialized Medicine," produced by the American Medical Association, 1961.

Reid, T. R. "Sick Around the World," *Frontline*, PBS, April 15, 2008, www. pbs.org/wgbh/pages/frontline/sickaroundtheworld/

Schorr, Daniel. "National Health Insurance," *CBS News*, February 18, 1971.

Shortall, Keith. "Obama Addresses Enthusiastic Crowd at the Portland Expo," *Maine Things Considered*, April 1, 2010.

YouTube, www.youtube.com Various videos.

ARTICLES

Adams, Damon. "Reagan Praised as Medicine's Friend," *American Medical News*, American Medical Association, June 21, 2004.

Adamy, Janet, and Naftali Bendavid. "House Passes Health-Care Reform Bill in Historic Vote," *Wall Street Journal*, November 8, 2009.

Allen, Jared. "Obama Slams Anthem Rate Increase in Pushing Healthcare Bill," *The Hill*, February 20, 2010.

Alonso-Zaldivar, Ricardo. "Two Parties, Two Remedies for Healthcare," *Los Angeles Times*, May 5, 2008.

Calman, Neil. "Making Health Equality a Reality: The Bronx Takes Action," *Health Affairs*, 24:2, 2005.

"Clinton Timeline," *MacNeil/Lehrer NewsHour*, PBS, 1996.

Congressional Record, 111th Cong., 1st sess., House, November 7, 2009, H12835–12836.

Conway, Laura. "Obama Says His Health Plan Won't 'Pull the Plug on Grandma,'" *Planet Money*, National Public Radio, August 11, 2009.

Corning, Peter A. "The Evolution of Medicare . . . from idea to law," Social Security Administration, 1969, www.ssa.gov/history/corning.html

Dickerson, John. "Death of a Salesman," *Slate*, July 13, 2010.

Dorn, Stan. "Uninsured and Dying Because of It: Updating the Institute of Medicine Analysis on the Impact of Uninsurance on Mortality," The Urban Institute: Washington, DC, January 8, 2008.

Editorial. "American Medical Association Joins American Hospital Association in Approving Pre-payment Medical as well as Hospital Service," *Journal of the National Medical Association*, 30:4, November 1938.

Ely, Richard T. "Economic Theory and Labor Legislation," *Proceedings of the First Annual Meeting of the American Association for Labor Legislation*, December 30–31, 1907.

"Employer Health Benefits, 2009 Annual Survey," Kaiser Family Foundation and Health Research & Educational Trust, #7936.

Fallows, James. "A Triumph of Misinformation," *The Atlantic*, January 1995.

"Fifth Annual Report of the Directors of the Maine General Hospital," Portland, ME: Stephen Berry, Printer, 1875.

Goldfarb, Walter B. "History of Surgery in Maine," *Archives of Surgery*, vol. 136, April 2001.

Goldfield, Norbert. "National health reform advocates retrench and prepare for Medicare," *Physician Executive*, May–June 1993.

Good, Chris. "No Conference for Health Bill . . . GOP Attacks to Follow," *The Atlantic*, January 4, 2010.

Goodwin, Sue. "American Cultural History: 1940–1949," Lone Star College–Kingwood Library, 1999.

Hall, Kevin G. "Democrats' health plans echo Nixon's failed GOP proposal," McClatchy Newspapers, November 28, 2007.

Hensel, Brian. "Harry Truman's reluctance in going public for national health insurance," paper presented at the annual meeting of the International Communication Association, New Orleans Sheraton, New Orleans, LA, May 27, 2004.

"Highlights from Obama's health care summit," CNN, February 25, 2010.

"History of BlueCross BlueShield Association, BCBSA website, www.bcbs.com/about/history/1920s.html, 2009.

"The History of Johns Hopkins Medicine," Johns Hopkins Medicine website, www.hopkinsmedicine.org/about/history/index.html

Hoffman, Beatrix. "Health Care Reform and Social Movements in the United States," *American Journal of Public Health*, January 2003, 93:1.

"House Passes Historic Health Care Reform Bill," PBS *NewsHour*, November 7, 2009.

Jackson, Jill, and John Nolen. "Health Care Reform Bill Summary: A Look at What's in the Bill." *CBS News*, March 23, 2010, www.cbsnews.com/8301-503544_162-20000846-503544.html

Jones, Ronald Coy. "History of the Department of Surgery at Baylor University Medical Center," *Baylor University Medical Center Proceedings*, April 2004.

Kapp, Matt. "The Sick Business of Health-Care Profiteering," *Vanity Fair*, September 24, 2009, www.vanityfair.com/politics/features/2009/09/health-care200909

Kettleborough, Charles, ed. "Legislative Notes and Reviews," *The American Political Science Review*, February 1919, 13:1.

Kiely, Kathy. "Senate passes health care bill," *USA Today*, December 25, 2009.

Lasseter, Francis. "A nursing legacy—political activities at the turn of the century," *AORN Journal*, November 1999.

Lepore, Jill. "Preexisting Condition," *The New Yorker*, December 7, 2009.

Levey, Noam N., and Janet Hook. "House passes historic healthcase overhaul," *Los Angeles Times*, March 22, 2010.

Maine General Hospital sample receipts, December 10–22, 1917.

Malcolm, Andrew. "The good news behind Obama's sad Natoma Canfield story," *Los Angeles Times*, March 16, 2010.

"National Health Expenditure Projections 2008–2018," Centers for Medicare and Medicaid Services, www.cms.gov/NationalHealthExpendData/downloads/proj2008.pdf

"National Health Insurance—A Brief History of Reform Efforts in the U.S.," *Focus on Health Reform*, Kaiser Family Foundation, March 2009.

"Natoma Canfield's letter," *The Columbus Dispatch*, March 15, 2010.

"New Haven's Hospitals," exhibit, Cushing/Whitney Medical Library, May 2000.

New York Times. Various articles (listed under Notes).

Nicholas, Peter, and Christi Parsons. "President Obama signs healthcare overhaul into law," *Los Angeles Times*, March 24, 2010.

Nolte, Ellen, and C. Martin McKee. "Measuring the Health of Nations: Updating an Earlier Analysis," *Health Affairs*, January/February 2008.

"Obama wins with speech-watchers, poll says," CNN, September 10, 2009.

"Overview of the Uninsured in the United States: An analysis of the 2005 Current Population Survey," U.S. Department of Health and Human Services, September 22, 2005.

Palmer, Karen S. "A Brief History: Universal Health Care Efforts in the U.S.," Physicians for a National Health Program, Spring 1999.

"President Harry S. Truman's Federal Health Insurance Plan," *California and Western Medicine*, 63:6, December 1945.

Roberts, Michelle. "Racial and Ethnic Differences in Health Insurance Coverage and Usual Source of Health Care, 2002." Rockville, MD: Agency of Healthcare Research and Quality, 2006.

Robeznieks, Andis. "AMA profit grows despite membership decline," *Modern Physician*, June 7, 2010.

Ross, Joseph S. "The Committee on the Costs of Medical Care and the History of Health Insurance in the United States," *Einstein Quarterly*, 19. 2002.

Rushing, J. Taylor. "Reid, Baucus ready to split on public option for healthcare as vote nears," *The Hill*, October 5, 2009.

Sahadi, Jeanne. "How Obama wants to pay for health reform," CNNMoney.com, February 22, 2010.

Scandlen, Greg. "Defined Contribution Health Insurance," National Center for Policy Analysis, No. 154, October 26, 2000, http://www.ncpa.org/pub/bg154

"Scrap Health Care Reform If It Adds to Deficit, U.S. Voters Tell Quinnipiac University National Poll," Quinnipiac University, August 5, 2009.

"Social Security History," Social Security Online History Pages, www.ssa.gov/history/corningchap3.html

Starr, Paul. "What Happened to Health Care Reform?" *The American Prospect*, no. 20, Winter 1995, 20–31.

"The Story of the Creation of the Nation's First Hospital," Penn Medicine, www.uphs.upenn.edu/paharc/features/creation.html

Tapper, Jake. "Palin Paints Picture of 'Obama Death Panel' Giving Thumbs Down to Trig," *ABC News*, August 7, 2009.

"Timeline: When health care reform will affect you," CNN, March 26, 2010.

Times Topics: "Health Care Reform," *New York Times*, July 1, 2010, http://topics.nytimes.com/top/news/health/diseasesconditionsandhealthtopics/health_insurance_and_managed_care/health_care_reform/index.html?scp=1-spot&sq= Health%20Care%20Reform&st=cse

"2008 Presidential Candidate Health Care Proposals: Side-by-Side Summary," health08.0rg, Kaiser Family Foundation.

"Welfare: Aid for the Aged," *Time* magazine, April 4, 1960.

"When Kennedy Nearly Achieved the 'Cause of His Life': Health Care Reform with Nixon," *Huffington Post*, August 26, 2009.

Will, George. "The Clintons' Lethal Paternalism," Newsweek, February 7, 1994.

Books

Daschle, Thomas. *Critical: What We Can Do About the Health-care Crisis.* New York: Thomas Dunne Books, 2008.

Gold, Susan Dudley. *The History of Maine Medical Center,* unpublished history. Portland, ME: Maine Health, 2001.

Gordon, Colin. *Dead on Arrival,* Princeton, NJ: Princeton University Press, 2004.

Hoffman, Beatrix. *The Wages of Sickness: The Politics of Health Insurance in Progressive America.* Chapel Hill: University of North Carolina Press, 2001.

Kirkendall, Richard S., ed. *The Harry S. Truman Encyclopedia.* Boston: G. K. Hall & Co., 1989.

Leavitt, Judith Walzer, and Ronald L. Numbers, eds. *Sickness and Health in America: Readings in the History of Medicine and Public Health.* Madison: University of Wisconsin Press, 1997.

Poen, Monte M. *Harry S. Truman Versus the Medical Lobby: The Genesis of Medicare.* Columbia: University of Missouri, 1979.

Smith, Jean Edward. *FDR.* New York: Random House, 2007.

Thompson, John D. and Grace Golden, *The Hospital: A Social and Architectural History.* New Haven: Yale University, 1975.

Updegrove, Mark K. *Second Acts: Presidential Lives and Legacies after the White House.* Guilford, CT: Lyons Press, 2006.

Watson, Robert W. *White House Studies Compendium,* vol. 5. New York: Nova Science Publishers Inc., 2008.

Documents, Graphs, Speeches, and Other Materials

"CHIP Ever Enrolled Year Graph." Centers for Medicare & Medicaid Services, www.cms.gov/NationalCHIPPolicy

Clark, Dean. "Is Your Health the Nation's Business? Constructing a Postwar World: The G.I. Roundtable Series in Context," American Historical Association for the Division of Information and Education, U.S. Army, pamphlet, January 1946.

Roosevelt, Theodore. "Address by Theodore Roosevelt Before the Convention of the National Progressive Party," Chicago, August 1912.

WEBSITES

Agency of Healthcare Research and Quality
www.ahrq.gov

American Medical Association
www.ama-assn.org

American Presidency Project
www.presidency.ucsb.edu

Centers for Medicare and Medicaid Services
www.cms.gov

DATA.gov
Access to government data via the Internet
www.data.gov

Kaiser Family Foundation
kff.org

National Center for Biotechnology Information
www.ncbi.nlm.nih.gov

National Institutes of Health
www.nih.gov

Social Security Administration
www.ssa.gov

Thomas, Library of Congress legislative information
http://thomas.loc.gov

U.S. Government Site on Health Care Reform Act Provisions
www.HealthCare.gov

White House
www.whitehouse.gov

All websites were accurate and accessible as of February 4, 2011.

Index

Page numbers in **boldface** are illustrations.

About the Author

Susan Dudley Gold has worked as a reporter for a daily newspaper, managing editor of two statewide business magazines, and freelance writer for several regional publications. She has written more than four dozen books for middle-school and high-school students on a variety of topics, including American history, health issues, law, and space.

Gold has won numerous awards for her work, including most recently the selection of *Loving* v. *Virginia: Lifting the Ban Against Interracial Marriage*, part of Marshall Cavendish's Supreme Court Milestones series, as one of the Notable Social Studies Trade Books for Young People in 2009. Three other books in that series have received recognition: *United States* v. *Amistad: Slave Ship Mutiny,* selected as a Carter G. Woodson Honor Book in 2008; and *Tinker* v. *Des Moines: Free Speech for Students* in 2008 and *Roberts* v. *Jaycees: Women's Rights* in 2010, both awarded first place in the National Federation of Press Women's communications contest, nonfiction juvenile book category.

Gold has written several titles in the Landmark Legislation series for Marshall Cavendish. She is the author of a number of books on Maine history. She and her husband, John Gold, own and operate a web design and publishing business in Maine. They have one son, Samuel; a granddaughter, Callie; and a grandson, Alexander.